W9-CEG-611

5664

GV
867.5   Appel
.A66   The first book of
1988   baseball

DATE DUE

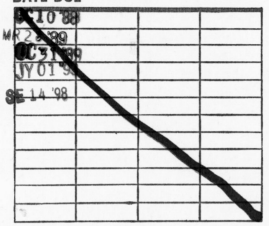

DE 10 '88			
MR 2 ' 89			
OC 3 ' 89			
JY 01 '9			
SE 14 '98			

The First Book Of Baseball
GV867.5.A66 1988   5664

Appel, Martin
VRJC/WRIGHT LIBRARY

DEMCO

The First Book of Baseball

MARTY APPEL

CROWN PUBLISHERS, INC.,
New York

VRJC LIBRARY

To Brian Jon Appel
whose question, "Why is the ball so hard?"
first inspired this book

Text Copyright © 1988 by Marty Appel

Title page drawing © June Gaddy.

Photos courtesy: Boston Red Sox (10, 34, 53), California Angels (64), Chicago White Sox (66), Cincinnati Reds (65), Houston Astros (12), Los Angeles Dodgers (54, 56), New York Yankees (47, 52, 53, 55, 57, 58, 59), St. Louis Cardinals (17).

Baseball cards © Topps Chewing Gum Company (55, 58, 61, 62, 63).

Lyrics from "Take Me Out to the Ballgame" (73) words by Jack Norwich.

All rights reserved. No part of this book may be reproduced or transmitted in any form or by any means, electronic or mechanical, including photocopying, recording, or by any information storage and retrieval system, without permission in writing from the publisher. Published by Crown Publishers, Inc., 225 Park Avenue South, New York, New York 10003 and represented in Canada by the Canadian MANDA Group. CROWN is a trademark of Crown Publishers, Inc.
Manufactured in the United States of America

Library of Congress Catalog Card Number 88-47653

ISBN 0-517-56726-1

10 9 8 7 6 5 4 3 2 1

First Edition

Front and back cover photographs © Chuck Solomon

Contents

The Elysian Fields, Hoboken, New Jersey, where the Knickerbockers lost to the New York Nine, June 19, 1846.

Thank You, Alex:

THE INVENTION OF BASEBALL

It was a lucky thing that Alexander Cartwright wasn't a sore loser.

Because if he were . . .

- There might be no baseball today
- No baseball cards to collect and trade
- No favorite teams to root for
- No favorite players to cheer for
- No box scores to read in the newspapers
- No family outings at the stadium
- No Little League games to play in
- No playing catch after school
- No World Series to get excited over

Instead of baseball being our "national pastime," it could have been rock collecting! Or spelling bees!

If Alexander Cartwright had been a sore loser, he just might have picked up his baseball, gone home, and forgotten all about this little gem of a game he had invented.

You see, Alexander may not have been the first person to think about hitting a ball with a stick, but he was the first to write down rules and put together a team to play by those rules. He called the team the

Knickerbockers. And when he had his rules, and he had his team, and he had them all suited up in their fancy new knicker-style uniforms, he challenged another bunch of guys to the first official game.

And the Knickerbockers lost, 23–1.

Now someone else might have yelled "never mind," and canceled the game. And someone else might have run onto the field and yelled to the umpire, "Wait, I invented this game, and I say whoever scores the *fewest* runs wins!" But Alexander Cartwright was a gentleman of honor and a good sport. He took the loss in good spirits and went out and tried again. And before long, the Knickerbockers got a little better and started to win. And other towns started to hear about them and put teams together to play them. And one town would challenge another. And before long, baseball was off and rolling, with teams appearing all over to represent their towns.

This was all back in the middle of the nineteenth century. Cartwright, a handsome, bearded volunteer fireman from New York, would row across the Hudson River with his friends and play on a beautiful field in Hoboken, New Jersey. It was Cartwright who decided what size the ball should be, the shape of the field, how runs were scored, how many feet the bases would be set apart, how many outs would make up an inning, how many strikes would make

Alexander Cartwright,
baseball's founding father.

up an out, and many of the other things that are still part of baseball today.

Little could Cartwright realize what he had created. What would he think if he were to return today and see some players making more than a million dollars a year to play his game? Or some 80 million people watching the World Series on something called television? Or baseball being played in so many countries besides the United States?

It sure was a lucky thing that Alexander Cartwright wasn't a sore loser.

It's How You Play the Game

To win at baseball, three things have to work together. When your team is at bat, you have to score runs. Sometimes you can win a game 1–0 but usually you need a few runs to win.

Next, your pitching has to be good. Your pitchers have to keep the opposing batters from socking the baseballs over the walls. If they can keep them from doing that, chances are the fielders will make the catches to get your opponents out.

And that is the third thing you need—good fielding. Everyone on the field has to be able to catch and throw and get the other side out. You can't expect your pitcher to strike out every batter he faces.

SCORING RUNS: BATTING AND BASERUNNING

You don't have to be a home-run slugger to be a good hitter. Many fine hitters have great value to their teams just by getting on base a lot, or helping to advance runners.

Power hitters tend to strike out a lot because they take big swings and often miss the ball completely. A lot of teams over the years have had great home-

THE FIRST BOOK OF BASEBALL

run hitters but no championships to show for it. Home runs aren't everything. They can bring in runs quickly, but this kind of speed doesn't count—there is no clock ticking away on a baseball scoreboard. Singles, a sacrifice bunt, walks, and doubles can also result in the same number of runs.

A good batting eye is the secret. If you swing at bad pitches, you will be cheating yourself out of walks and either missing the ball completely or hitting it weakly.

Basically:

- If you hit the *top* part of the ball, it will result in a grounder.
- Hitting the *middle* of the ball will result in a line drive.
- Hitting the *bottom* part of the ball will result in a fly ball.
- Hitting the *underside* of the ball results in a foul back, or a foul tip.

That's easy to say, but with major-league pitches at ninety or a hundred miles an hour that curve or drop in the strike zone, it is hard to be that perfect in hitting the ball. Still with a keen batting eye, and a lot of practice, a batter could improve the number of line drives he hits, and they are always the best chance for getting on base.

Helping to advance the baserunners can take exceptional bat control. This is accomplished by the positioning of a batter's legs and the timing of his swing.

Wade Boggs—a great batting eye in practice.

With a runner on second, for example, a good batter will hit the ball toward the first-base side of the field, in order to advance the runner to third. If he hits it on to the third-base side, the runner on second will usually have to stay put.

Even if the batter makes an out, he'll receive a lot of slaps on the back in the dugout when he does his job and moves the runner along. A runner on third is just ninety feet away from scoring a run.

Here's another example. With a runner on first base, the pitcher will try to *make* the batter hit the top part of the ball. The pitcher wants the batter to ground into a double play, and the batter wants to advance the runner. Every pitch is a battle between the pitcher and batter.

THE FIRST BOOK OF BASEBALL

Baserunners can try to "steal" the next base at any time they wish when the ball is "live," or in play. Stealing a base means that a baserunner goes for the next base all on his own.

The best time to steal is just as the pitcher releases the ball. That gives the runner the most time to get to a base before a play can be made.

Second base is the easiest base to steal because it is the longest throw for a catcher (second is a little more than 127 feet from home plate). Home plate is the hardest to steal because the catcher is right there waiting with the ball, but home plate *has* been stolen. It takes a great slide and a bit of surprise. Sometimes it comes as part of a double steal, in which two runners take off at the same time. If the catcher fires the ball to second, the runner on third might just try to steal home.

Good baserunners are not only fast ones. The ones who have good feelings for when to go for an extra base, when to hold up where they are, and how to slide to avoid a tag can help a team, too.

PITCHING

Many people feel that pitching is the most important part of a team. Usually, a good pitching performance will stop good hitting.

The pitcher's job is to throw strikes. A pitch is a strike when

- the batter swings and misses any pitch
- the pitch is hit into foul territory

• an umpire behind home plate rules that the pitch was in the batter's **strike zone**

The strike zone is over home plate, and between the batter's knee and midchest.

Three strikes make a **strikeout.**

A pitch thrown *outside* the strike zone is a **ball.** Four balls, and the batter gets to go to first base. This is called a **base on balls,** or a **walk.** Balls and strikes are both called by the home plate umpire. When a pitcher throws a strike, the umpire raises his right hand. On a ball, he doesn't raise his hand at all.

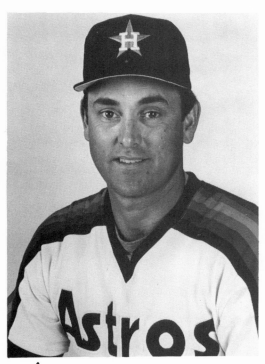

Baseball's all-time strike-out king, Nolan Ryan.

THE FIRST BOOK OF BASEBALL

> *A special note about foul balls:* Umpires on the field judge whether a ball was hit fair or foul. A foul ball can count as strikes one and two, but not as strike three except under certain circumstances.
>
> Fouls only count as strike three when
> - you bunt with two strikes against you and the bunted ball goes foul
> - you hit a foul tip (a ball hit straight back at the catcher) with two strikes against you and the catcher catches it

The pitcher must work very carefully with his catcher in figuring how to "work" a hitter.

Most batters have weaknesses and strengths. If a batter has trouble hitting low, inside strikes, for instance, that's what the pitcher will throw. A good pitcher–catcher battery can be a beautiful thing to watch.

Pitchers throw a variety of pitches to keep the batters off-balance and guessing about what might be coming next. Fooling the batter is an important part in deciding which pitch to throw.

Most successful pitchers can throw **fastballs, change-ups,** and **breaking pitches** to keep batters fooled.

- Fastballs are especially effective if they have a little movement to them, such as a *rise* or a *drop* as they get near home plate.
- Change-ups are slower pitches. If the batter is timing his swing to hit a fastball, his swing will be way out in front of a change-up.

- Breaking pitches can be curveballs, sliders, screwballs, knuckleballs, split-fingered fastballs, or anything a pitcher might come up with that dances a little on its way to the plate. (Legally, that is. A ball scuffed with sandpaper, for example, dances—but the rules prohibit any "doctoring" of the ball.)

Breaking pitches are thrown by using the seams on the ball and positioning the fingers across them, or with them, to give the pitch movement. A wrist snap in the delivery is often part of the success of these tricky pitches.

The human arm is designed to swing underhanded. Pitching overhand is an unnatural motion, and most pitchers get sore arms sooner or later. Some manage to postpone this for as long as fifteen to twenty years, but some get sore arms early in their careers, and a lot of promise is down the drain. That's why it is always difficult to be certain if a pitcher will have a long and successful career, and why youngsters are not encouraged to throw breaking balls before their arms are fully developed.

Starting pitchers in the major leagues usually work every fourth or fifth day and try to go seven innings or more. After the seventh, a fresh relief pitcher might come in from the bullpen (the place where relief pitchers warm up). If the relief pitcher throws mostly fastballs, and the starting pitcher has been using breaking pitches, the batters may have an extra hard time adjusting to the change.

Relief pitchers also come into the game (at any inning) when the starting pitcher is having trouble. Once any player, including a pitcher, leaves a game he can't come back. It's shower time for him. Removing a pitcher is a *big* decision.

If a dangerous right-handed batter is at the plate in a game-winning situation, the manager may want to bring in a *right-handed* relief pitcher from the bullpen.

Curveballs thrown left handed break to the right. And curveballs thrown right handed break to the left. A right-handed pitcher has an advantage against a right-handed batter, and a left-handed pitcher has an advantage against a left-handed batter, because their curveballs break *away* from the hitter. A pitch that comes toward you is much easier to hit than one that's moving away from you.

Managers often change their batting orders, depending on which way the opposing pitcher throws. If a manager has two second basemen, a right hander and a left hander, the right hander is likely to see action against left-handed pitchers. This system is called *platooning* players. A switch-hitter, one who can hit either righty or lefty, is very valuable and will see more playing time. Mickey Mantle, Pete Rose, and Eddie Murray are three of the more successful switch-hitters of recent history.

A smart pitcher keeps baserunners close to their bases, so they won't get too much of a head start trying to steal, or gain an extra base if a ball is hit.

Pitchers throw to first a lot when there is a speedy runner on that base, trying to pick him off for an out, or at least keep him close to the bag.

Pitchers must be careful to avoid **balks,** which the umpires call when a pitcher makes an illegal motion (see Glossary for more on balks). On a balk, all runners advance one base.

Pitchers must also avoid **wild pitches.** If a pitch is "wild," and gets past the catcher, the ball is in play and runners can take as many bases as they're able to.

The difference between a wild pitch and passed ball is that a wild pitch is the pitcher's fault. A passed ball is also a pitch that gets past the catcher, but the official scorer rules that the catcher should have caught it.

The pitcher also has to remember that he is a fielder, too. If a ball is hit toward first, and the first basemen leaves his base to field the ball, the pitcher must run over and cover the bag. If a ball gets past the catcher with an opposing runner on third, the pitcher must cover home plate. He also should back up other fielders on throws coming from the outfield in case of overthrows.

FIELDING

Different fielding positions require different skills, but all positions require quick thinking. Fielders have to be ready for anything. Before every

A baserunner like Vince Coleman gives opposing infielders another thing to think about—a stolen base.

pitch, a fielder must be thinking, *"What do I do if the ball is hit to me?"*

Catching the ball is one thing. Knowing where to throw it is something else. A throw to a wrong base or forgetting how many outs there are can cost your team the game.

If you struck out your last time at bat with the bases loaded, you have to put it out of your mind when you go into the field. You have a new job to do out there and you can't let your teammates down.

Fly balls and pop-ups give fielders the longest time to prepare for the catch, but that also presents the possibility of two fielders crashing into each other. That is why a smart fielder will shout, "I've got it, I've got it!" as he circles under the ball.

Two fielders, both yelling "I've got it," will probably result in the ball dropping between them. That's not so smart. Experience teaches good judgment on balls hit in the air.

A line drive doesn't leave time for yelling. The fielder has to react instantly and get his glove up. He has to know whether to back hand the ball or to take it on his glove side. Line drives sometimes give fielders a chance to make a quick double play if there's a baserunner. A fast and accurate throw can double up a runner who is too far off base.

Infielders get the most "hot" grounders, and they have to be quick on their feet to go after the ball. So many hot grounders (and hard-hit line drives) come near third base, that it's often called "the hot corner." Sharply hit grounders also offer a chance for a double play, or at least a force-out on a lead baserunner.

A **force-out** happens because two runners can't be on the same base. When a runner *has* to run for the next base because a batter has hit the ball and is taking the runner's base, the runner can be forced out. When a runner is forced to go to the next base (including home plate), a step on the base by a fielder with the ball will force the runner out. No tag is necessary.

Before the pitch, in any situation, know which base you're going to throw to. Know if you have to tag a runner or if you can just step on the base and force him out.

For a fielder, knowing where to *play* the hitters is as important as being quick. Remembering where the batter hit the ball his last times at the plate can help a fielder position himself—and it might even save a game.

Footwork is important in fielding, especially in receiving throws from your teammates. If you're catching a throw at a base, make sure your foot stays on the base until the catch is made. Second basemen have the trickiest footwork on the field, because they have to remember to make a full turn on many double play attempts and have to remember to get out of the way of sliding runners.

The best fielders are not always the ones with the fewest errors. The best fielders are aggressive on the field and go after whatever they can reach. If you can make the play—make it! Fielders who play it safe make few errors, but seldom make the big play when it is needed. They are the ones who "let the ball play them," and back up for grounders or let other players make diving catches. A manager would much rather have a fielder who isn't afraid to get his uniform dirty scrambling after anything hit near him.

In the major leagues, the best fielders at each position are awarded Gold Gloves at the end of the season. The award has very little to do with the number of errors the fielders make. It is mostly what people think of a fielder's ability to take charge on the field and make the hard plays. Everyone makes

VRJC LIBRARY

errors, and when you make one, don't sulk, kick the dirt, or blame a pebble. Keep your head up and make up for it the next time the ball is hit to you. And don't make a teammate feel badly either. Pat him on the back when you trot off the field together and tell him, "You'll get 'em next time."

Teamwork is probably more important in fielding that in any other part of the game. A good team must know where everyone moves whenever a ball is hit. Who backs up which base, who covers first, who moves in to take the cutoff throw from the outfield, and other points are important to practice *before* a season begins. The best teams are the ones that make the right plays the most often. Sloppy teamwork leads to defeat. A player can accept a defeat if the opposing pitcher hurls a great game or if the opponents have a big day at bat, but to lose a game because the team did not know how to play good fundamental baseball is a painful thing.

HOW A SINGLE GAME IS PLAYED

A game is divided into **innings.** Each team stays at bat until they have made **three outs.** When both teams have made three outs, that makes one inning.

Major-league games last nine innings. It *can* be shorter if it rains (a game has to go at least five innings for it to be an official, complete game), or longer if the score is tied in the ninth inning. Beyond the ninth, it's called **extra innings.** There is no time limit to a game.

THE FIRST BOOK OF BASEBALL

The manager selects players for each position and also selects the **batting order** (the order in which the players will come to bat when the opposing team is on the field—also called *the lineup*). Fast runners who get on base a lot usually bat in the first spots, power hitters bat in the middle, and less reliable hitters in the bottom part. If all the hitters are "less reliable," and there is no speed or power, this is probably not going to be a great season.

Players must stay in their batting order throughout the game. When an inning is over, the next inning will begin with the player who was supposed to bat next (the batter who was **on deck**).

The **home team** is in the field first. This means they bat last, and will always get the "last licks" to win the game.

Visitors bat in the top half of an inning and the home team in the bottom half. If the home team is winning after the top half of the ninth has been played, there is no need for them to bat in the last half of the ninth. They've already won the game.

This is how the defense stands when they're fielding their positions.

They may shift (or **shade**) a little bit one way or the other, or move back or come in, depending on who is batting. If the batter is a power hitter, the outfielders may stand farther back. If the batter hits lefty, everyone may shade a little bit toward the rightfield side. If he's a righty, they shade to the leftfield side.

Batters naturally **pull** the ball, drive it in the direction their bats swing. Lefties pull the ball to right field. Righties pull the ball to left field.

When a batter doesn't pull the ball, it's called hitting to the **opposite field.** That's when a left-handed batter hits to left field or a right-handed batter hits to right field. An opposite field home run might be when a right-handed batter hits the ball over the right field fence.

The team scoring first will try to stop the other team from tying the score. As the game progresses, the team with the lead might send in **defensive replacements** for players who hit better than they field. These substitutes might replace better hitters, but good fielding is more important when you're protecting a lead. An error could cost you the game.

The team might also protect its lead by bringing a relief pitcher out of the bullpen, fresh and full of energy, to stop a **rally** by the losing team (a "rally" is when a team is getting on base and threatening to score, or is scoring).

Teams may also use **pinch-hitters** and **pinch-runners** to try and gain an advantage. Pinch-hitters bat for a teammate, and pinch-runners run for one who has gotten on base. Remember, though, once a player leaves the game . . . he can't return.

Eventually, the game will end with one team having scored more runs—the object of the game.

What Happens in a Baseball Season

For some people the new year begins on January 1st. But for millions of baseball fans, the new year begins in February. They call it a new "season" and they measure years by the passing of the baseball seasons. Even though it is still winter, baseball is in the air.

New baseball magazines are in the stores. On the covers are beautiful color photographs of last year's best players. Or perhaps there is a photo of the world champions celebrating their World Series victory.

The first baseball cards appear in the candy stores. What will their design be this year? Can we collect the whole set? Should we just try to collect players from our favorite team? How great they smell when they come wrapped with bubble gum!

Maybe this season will be a good one to visit a card show and try to buy some old cards and start a collection.

Now comes a day of melting snow and a touch of warm weather. What a perfect day to get out the old mitt and have the first catch of the season with a friend. The arms feel a little stiff, and we don't want to overdo it, but the sound of baseballs snapping into leather gloves lets us know that spring is in the air and the baseball season can't be far behind.

FEBRUARY: SPRING TRAINING BEGINS

All over the country, players are packing up their spikes and mitts and heading for spring training camps.

Every major-league club also operates five or six minor-league teams in cities and towns across America.

The minor-league players are off to spring training, too. Maybe they will need a few more seasons of work to become good enough for the big leagues. Or maybe this is their year! Maybe they will play so well in spring training that the manager will just *have* to bring them up to the major-league team.

Some players never reach the majors after all. But at least they will have tried.

Stories begin to appear in the newspapers about the training camps. Who are the best rookies? Will last year's championship teams be just as good this year? Which players are trying to come back after an injury last season? How will new players on teams work out?

Pictures from sunny Florida and Arizona show

the players working hard to get in shape for the new season. They do exercises, and go through batting, fielding, and pitching drills. They also play preseason exhibition games against other teams. These games are called the **Grapefruit League** in Florida and the **Cactus League** in Arizona.

Practice is not just for Little Leaguers. Even grownups playing professional baseball have to eat the right foods, get plenty of rest, and train long and hard to be in top form.

Most major-league players are between twenty and forty years old. Most are between 5 feet 10 inches tall and 6 feet 4 inches tall, and weigh between 170 and 225 pounds. Some are from big cities, some are from small towns. Some went to college, some signed a pro contract right out of high school. Some have families, some are single. Most are from the United States, but a lot of players come from Puerto Rico, the Dominican Republic, Mexico, and Canada. The teams that they play for have little to do with the towns they come from. But during the season, everyone in town treats the "home town" player just like he was one of their very own.

By the beginning of April, the managers are sending some players to the minors and letting others go, in order to be ready for **opening day** (the first official game of the season). **Rosters** (the list of players a team can use during a game) for major-league teams are made up of twenty-four players.

Most teams have about nine pitchers—four starting pitchers, four relief pitchers, and one who can do either if necessary. They usually have two catchers, about eight infielders, and about six outfielders. In the American League, one of the outfielders is usually considered a designated hitter, someone who will play very little (if at all) in the field and mostly just bat in place of the pitcher.

The **regulars** on any team are the players who are in the lineup almost every day (unless they are injured). The **reserves** are the players who are always ready to take over for the regulars. They may be called on to pinch-hit, pinch-run, play the field, or replace an injured player. Most reserves would rather play regularly, and they have to take advantage of every opportunity to impress the manager and prove what they can do.

Lou Gehrig, for example, was a reserve player for the Yankees in 1923. The regular first baseman, Wally Pipp, told his manager he was too sick to play one day. Rookie Lou Gehrig was substituted in Pipp's place. And Gehrig didn't miss a game for the next fourteen years.

The final cuts in spring training are often the veteran players (players who have been in the big leagues for several years) who simply don't fit with the club any longer. Those are the hardest cuts for the manager to make, but he must put together his best possible team. After all, his job is to win. And a team that has a bad season might fire its manager and hire a new one. A bad season may not actually be a manager's fault, but an old saying goes, "It's easier to fire one manager than all of the players."

APRIL: THE START OF A NEW SEASON

Flags are flapping in the wind, and it's time once again for **opening day**. Every team starts out equally—no wins and no losses. Every team has an equal chance to win the **pennant** in its league, and to beat the other league's pennant winner in the **World Series.**

The public address announcer introduces all the players to the fans. The baselines and batter's box have clean white lines. The gentle spray of the groundskeeper's hose has turned the infield dirt dark brown. The field is peaceful, but there is excitement in the air.

Is the President of the United States throwing out the first ball of the season? Sometimes he does. The first one to do that was President Taft back in 1910. It was a lot easier when there was a team in Washington, but even now, Presidents will sometimes travel to the first game.

The Commissioner of Baseball is there, and so are the presidents of the American and National Leagues. At the home park of the world champions, each player is presented with a World Series ring. Pennants are raised just below the American flag in a special ceremony at the ballparks of last year's

National and American League pennant winners. It will not be easy to win another pennant. Teams play their best against the champions because they are anxious to beat the best.

Since baseball is played almost every day, the games start adding up quickly. **There are 162 games to play,** lots of time for the best teams to rise to the top and the worst teams to settle near the bottom.

Of the 162 games, each team plays half at home (81) and half on the road (81). The players wear different uniforms for home games or road games, usually bright white at home and light gray on the road. To make the pennant race fair, each team plays the same number of games against every other team. Nobody can win a pennant by playing an easier schedule. But a manager still has to plan his season carefully, and he has to have his best pitchers ready for the most important games—the games against tough teams in his own division. These are the games that really bring the fans out to the ball-park.

There are not too many days off during the season, and all the travel can make the players weary. Never a Saturday or Sunday off, never a summer vacation.

Each day the newspapers report the standings, the box scores, and the league leading statistics. A **batting average** (sometimes abbreviated as

Avg. or Pct.) tells you the percentage of hits per times **at bat.** A .364 hitter gets 364 per 1,000 at bats. Or, rounding it off, 36 hits per 100 at bats. *At bat* in this statistic doesn't mean every time the batter has come to the plate. For a walk, a hit by pitch, or a sacrifice, no *"at bat" is charge against the batter's batting average.* A batter who goes to the plate four times, gets a single, two walks, and a sacrifice is considered to have one hit in one at bat for the game.

A sacrifice can be two kinds of outs. First, there's a **sacrifice fly.**

Sacrifice flies happen when there is a runner on third and fewer than two outs. A batter hits the ball to the outfield and the ball is caught in flight— putting the batter out. Then the runner can **tag up** (step on the base after the catch) and run home.

Sacrifice bunts also help build runs. A good bunter can drop the ball gently in front of home plate, and while he will probably be thrown out at first, a teammate on base will have raced to the next base.

If a sacrifice bunt gets a teammate from first base to second, the runner is now in **scoring position.** A single to the outfield could drive him home.

A **fielding percentage** is a percentage of his errors per plays. A 1.000 fielding percentage is a perfect score. It means the fielder has committed no errors.

Even the best fielders fumble grounders, drop

fly balls, or make bad throws. It is up to an **official scorer** (a sportswriter in the press box) to rule whether a fielder made an error on a play.

An **earned run average** tells you how many *earned runs* (runs scored by baserunners who *didn't* get to base on an error—even the pitcher's) a pitcher gives up, on average, per nine innings. A baserunner who scores or reaches base and scores due to an error is an **unearned run.**

Early in the season, batting averages can change a lot from day to day, because the players haven't been to bat hundreds of times yet. When they have, their averages only change by one or two points a day.

The **standings** tell you how the clubs are ranked so far in the season. Who is in first place? Who is in last? Which teams are close to the top? Is there a game today between a first-place team and a second-place team? That can be an important game! A chance for the second-place team to catch up.

If a team can keep winning, no other team can gain any ground on it. But if the first-place team loses, every team that wins that day gains a game in the standings. If a team has a long winning streak or a long losing streak, it can gain or lose a lot of ground in a hurry.

The **box scores** give you almost every detail of a baseball game. Some fans glance at the box scores to see how their favorite players did. Others study

INDIVIDUAL BATTING
Leaders—Based on 502 plate appearances.

°Indicates rookie. †Bats lefthanded. ‡Switch-hitter.

Player—Club	Pct.	G.	AB.	R.	H.	2B.	3B.	HR.	RBI.	BB.	SO.	SB.
Gwynn, San Diego†	.370	157	589	119	218	36	13	7	54	82	35	56
Guerrero, Los Angeles	.338	152	545	89	184	25	2	27	89	74	85	9
Raines, Montreal‡	.330	139	530	123	175	34	8	18	68	90	52	50
Kruk, San Diego†	.313	138	447	72	140	14	2	20	91	73	93	18
James, Atlanta†	.312	134	494	80	154	37	6	10	61	70	63	10
Clark, San Francisco†	.308	150	529	89	163	29	5	35	91	49	98	5
Galarraga, Montreal	.305	147	551	72	168	40	3	13	90	41	127	7
Smith, St. Louis‡	.303	158	600	104	182	40	4	0	75	89	36	43
Thompson, Phila.†	.302	150	527	86	159	26	9	7	43	42	87	46
Bonilla, Pittsburgh‡	.300	141	466	58	140	33	3	15	.77	39	64	3
ATLANTA	Pct.	G.	AB.	R.	H.	2B.	3B.	HR.	RBI.	BB.	SO.	SB.

LEAGUE LEADERS—BATTING
Pct.—Batting Average (sometimes listed as Avg.), G—Games, AB—At Bats, R—Runs Scored, H—Hits, 2B—Doubles, 3B—Triples, HR—Home Runs, RBI—Runs Batted In, BB—Bases on Balls (sometimes listed as W for Walks), SO—Strikeouts, SB—Stolen Bases. Some listings also show number of Sacrifice Flies (SF), Sacrifice Hits (SH), times Hit by a Pitch (HBP), and times Caught Stealing (CS).

CATCHERS

Leader, Club	Pct.	G.	PO.	A.	E.	DP.	PB.
ASHBY, HOU.	.993	110	778	46	6	6	6

Player, Club	Pct.	G.	PO.	A.	E.	DP.	PB.
Ashby, Hou.	.993	110	778	46	6	6	6
Bailey, Hou.	.985	27	126	7	2	0	0
Benedict, Atl.	.989	35	165	21	2	3	1
Berryhill, Chi.	.909	11	37	3	4	0	0
Bochy, S.D.	.962	23	95	7	4	0	0
Brenly, S.F.	.988	108	642	83	9	10	11
Carter, N.Y.	.991	135	874	70	9	13	5
Daulton, Phil.	.991	40	200	12	2	4	1
J. Davis, Chi.	.989	123	749	79	9	11	12
Diaz, Cin.	.992	137	747	70	7	6	9
Lake, St.L.	.996	59	253	21	1	2	1
Fitzgerald, Mtl.	.981	104	602	27	12	2	4
LaValliere, Pitt.	.992	112	584	70	5	11	2
Lyons, N.Y.	.984	49	223	17	4	0	4
McClendon, Cin.	.981	12	49	4	1	1	2
McGriff, Cin.	.983	33	160	14	3	1	1
Melvin, S.F.	.998	78	407	43	1	7	4
Ortiz, Pitt.	.975	72	313	39	9	2	6
Pagnozzi, St.L.	1.000	25	53	4	0	0	1
Parrish, Phil.	.989	127	724	66	9	1	15
Pena, St.L.	.988	112	615	51	8	8	14
Reed, Mtl.	.970	74	357	36	12	6	4
R. Reynolds, Hou.	.975	38	216	16	6	1	1
Santiago, S.D.	.976	146	817	80	22	12	22
Scioscia, L.A.	.989	138	925	80	11	11	6
Simmons, Atl.	.987	15	64	10	1	1	2
Stefero, Mtl.	.981	17	90	12	2	0	0
Sundberg, Chi.	.994	57	273	34	2	2	1
Trevino, L.A.	.987	45	205	22	3	3	2
Virgil, Atl.	.989	122	654	74	8	12	8
Wine, Hou.	.979	12	40	7	1	2	1

LEAGUE LEADERS—DEFENSE BY POSITION
Pct.—Fielding Percentage, G—Games at that position, PO—Putouts, A—Assists, E—Errors, DP—Double Plays participated in, PB—Passed Balls (for catchers only).

MINNESOTA AT DETROIT (D)

Two-run homer by Sheridan in eighth inning enabled Tigers to edge Twins, 7-6, and cut Minnesota's series lead to 2-1.

Minnesota	ab	r	h	rbi	Detroit	ab	r	h	rbi
Gladden, lf	3	1	1	0	Whitaker, 2b	4	1	1	0
Gagne, ss	5	2	1	1	Evans, 1b	1	0	0	0
Puckett, cf	5	0	0	0	Gibson, lf	5	1	1	1
Hrbek, 1b	3	1	0	0	Trammell, ss	4	1	1	1
Gaetti, 3b	5	0	2	2	Nokes, c	3	0	0	0
Bush, dh	3	1	1	1	Lemon, cf	3	1	0	0
Brunansky, rf	3	1	1	2	Bergman, dh	1	0	0	0
L'b'dozzi, 2b	3	0	0	0	Herndon, dh	3	0	2	2
Butera, c	3	0	2	0	Morris, pr	0	1	0	0
Davidson, pr	0	0	0	0	Brookens, 3b	4	0	0	0
Laudner, c	1	0	0	0	Sheridan, rf	4	2	2	2
Totals	34	6	8	6	Totals	32	7	7	6

```
Minnesota ................0 0 0  2 0 2  2 0 0—6
Detroit ..................0 0 5  0 0 0  0 2 x—7
```

Minnesota	IP.	H.	R.	ER.	BB.	SO.
Straker	2⅔	3	5	5	4	1
Schatzeder	3⅓†	2	0	0	0	5
Berenguer	1	0	0	0	1	1
Reardon (Loser)	1	2	2	2	1	0

Detroit	IP.	H.	R.	ER.	BB.	SO.
Terrell	6*	7	6	6	4	4
Henneman (Winner)	3	1	0	0	3	1

*Pitched to two batters in seventh.
†Pitched to one batter in seventh.
Game-winning RBI—Sheridan.
E—Lombardozzi. LOB—Minnesota 8, Detroit 8. 2B—Sheridan, Herndon. HR—Gagne, Brunansky, Sheridan. SB—Gibson 2. HBP—By Schatzeder (Evans). Balk—Straker. T—3:29. A—49,730.

BOX SCORE
A box score shows what each batter did, the score by innings, what each pitcher did (every out counts as a third of an inning so if a pitcher leaves the game with two outs, he'll be credited with two thirds of an inning pitched), and a summary of other information, including runners Left on Base (LOB), time of game (T), and attendance (A).

INDIVIDUAL PITCHING
Leaders—Based on 162 innings.

°Indicates rookie status. †Throws lefthanded.

Pitcher—Club	W.	L.	ERA.	G.	GS.	CG.	ShO.	Sv.	IP.	H.	BB.	SO.
Ryan, Houston	8	16	2.76	34	34	0	0	0	211.2	154	87	270
°Dunne, Pittsburgh	13	6	3.03	23	23	5	1	0	163.1	143	68	72
Hershiser, Los Angeles	16	16	3.06	37	35	10	1	1	264.2	247	74	190
Reuschel, Pitts.-S.F.	13	9	3.09	34	33	12	4	0	227.0	207	42	107
Gooden, New York	15	7	3.21	25	25	7	3	0	179.2	162	53	148
Welch, Los Angeles	15	9	3.22	35	35	6	4	0	251.2	204	86	196
Scott, Houston	16	13	3.23	36	36	8	3	0	247.2	199	79	233
Dravecky, S.D.-S.F.†	7	12	3.43	48	28	5	3	0	191.1	186	64	138
°Magrane, St. Louis†	9	7	3.54	27	26	4	2	0	170.1	157	60	101
Hammaker, S. Fran.†	10	10	3.58	31	27	2	0	0	168.1	159	57	107

LEAGUE LEADERS—PITCHERS
W—Wins, L—Losses, ERA—Earned Run Average, G—Games Pitched, GS—Games Started, CG—Complete Games, ShO—Shutouts, Sv—Saves (sometimes listed as S), IP—Innings Pitched, H—Hits Allowed, BB—Bases on Balls Allowed (also W for Walks), SO—Strikeouts.

them long and hard. The box scores tell you many things including who hit home runs or stole bases, and, after their names, how many homers or steals they have for the season. For pitchers, the box scores tells you who the winning and losing pitchers were and what their records are for the season.

Although every player participates in helping his team win or lose, only a pitcher gets personal credit for a win or loss. A starting pitcher must pitch at least five innings and leave the game with his team ahead to get the win. If the score is tied when the starting pitcher leaves, the relief pitcher might get the win. The loss goes to the pitcher who was on the mound when his team fell behind—no matter what inning—when his team loses the game.

A relief pitcher may also be credited with a **save** if he holds on to a lead and finishes a game.

Managers like to study box scores of the teams that they will be playing in a few days. They can see which hitters are "hot," which ones are in a slump, and which starting pitchers they are likely to face.

MAY

In early May, some teams have gotten off to fast starts, and others haven't. Are there any surprise teams out in front? Did sportswriters and fans think that a certain team would finish in last place, and actually it's in first place? Baseball is full of surprises, but there is a long way to go.

Which players are off to fast starts? Is anyone belting home runs at a "record pace"? Does any player have a chance, even this early in the year, to break Roger Maris's record of sixty-one home runs in one season?

By the end of May, fans are voting for the **All-Star** teams. They can select one player at each position. Choosing the pitchers is left to the team managers and league offices. Which players should we vote for? Players who had a great season last year? Players who are off to fast starts this season? Players who have had long and great careers?

There is no right or wrong answer to this. A fan can choose whomever he wants—even his favorite player, even if his favorite player is having a terrible season. It's a game for the fans, and they can vote any way they want to.

The All-Star Game itself is played in a different city each year. Every major-league team has to have at least one of its players on the All-Star team. It is the American League against the National League, and a chance to see all the great stars on one field at the same time. Look at all those different uniforms! How strange it is to see. It is the only game all season, besides spring training and the World Series, when the two leagues play against each other.

The game doesn't count in the standings, and those players who weren't selected to the team have three days off to rest up for the second half of the season. Those chosen are honored to be picked and try to help their league win. In baseball, more than in any other sport, the rivalry between the two leagues is strong.

JULY

After the All-Star break, the pennant races really heat up. Baseball fever! Attendance records are broken as top teams face each other. Which pitchers will win 20 games this season? Who will be the batting, home run, and RBI champions? To win all three is called winning the Triple Crown. That doesn't happen very often.

Are there any milestones which will be set this

TRIPLE CROWN WINNERS
American League
1909   Ty Cobb, Detroit
1933   Jimmie Foxx, Philadelphia
1934   Lou Gehrig, New York
1942   Ted Williams, Boston
1947   Ted Williams, Boston
1956   Mickey Mantle, New York
1966   Frank Robinson, Baltimore
1967   Carl Yastrzemski, Boston

National League
1912   Heinie Zimmerman, Chicago
1922   Rogers Hornsby, St. Louis
1925   Rogers Hornsby, St. Louis
1933   Chuck Klein, Philadelphia
1937   Joe Medwick, St. Louis

"Yaz"—Carl Yastrzemski, the last man to accomplish the Triple Crown.

year? Will any pitcher win his 300th victory or will any batter record his 3,000th hit? Will anyone set a new record for stolen bases in one season? Will anyone pitch a no-hitter? A perfect game? Will anyone hit four home runs in a game?

SEPTEMBER–OCTOBER

In the final weeks of the season, teams usually play games only against their own division opponents. Writers and sportscasters talk of a "magic number"—the combination of wins by the first-place team and losses by the second-place team that, added together, will make it impossible for the second-place team to catch up.

One by one, the division champions celebrate clinching the title. But that's only the first step. **When the season ends, there are four division winners in quest of a world championship.** The Eastern and Western Divisions face each other in League Championship Series in each league. Fans often call these series "playoffs." That will leave two pennant winners, one from the American League and one from the National League, to meet in the World Series.

It's October. A chill has returned to the air. The players are wearing long-sleeved sweatshirts under their uniform tops. American flags are all over the ballparks. At home, millions of fans will be watching on television, even fans who paid little attention during the regular season. Suddenly, all the players in the World Series seem famous. Before it is over, we will know their habits, their superstitions, their families, their records. In a matter of about a week, the world championship will be decided. Right after the deciding game, there will be a wild celebration in the winners' clubhouse, then a parade in their home city, and a celebration at city hall. The star players will appear in department stores, speak at banquets, write books, and appear on television commercials.

The "off season" is filled with baseball news. Awards are presented. Players are named Most Valuable Player and Rookie of the Year in each league. The best pitchers win the Cy Young Award. There are awards for Manager of the Year and even Comeback Player of the Year for a player who bounced back from a bad season. Gold Gloves are announced for the best fielders.

Some players will be traded to new teams. Some will be sold to new teams. Some will be released, and their careers will be over. Some will be free agents and have the right to shop around for new teams of their own choosing, if those teams are interested in them. Players sign new contracts, some for more than $1 million a year! All for playing a game.

Elections are held for the Hall of Fame, the greatest honor a player can receive. He has to be retired for five seasons before the sportswriters can consider him. Fans love to talk about whether a certain player has a chance to make the Hall of Fame.

Some teams try to improve by adding many new players. If a team had a bad year, maybe its attendance was way down, and it lost a lot of money. Many teams give gifts to their fans on days like cap day, ball day, or bat day, but most of all, fans like to support winning teams. And so each team spends the winter months making whatever moves it can to improve over the past season.

January arrives. It's almost time for the Super Bowl, the final football game of the year. And once that game has been played, it's only a matter of weeks until spring training is here again, and the wonderful game called baseball, American's national pastime, is here with us all again.

Play ball!

A packed house waits for the action at Boston's Fenway Park.

SPALDING'S

League Ball and SPALDING'S Boys' League are the official BASE BALLS for the season of '99 and should be used in all games

OFFICIAL LEAGUE BALL.
Price $1.25.
Used exclusively by National League.
Postage 1c. additional.

BOYS' LEAGUE BALL. Price 75 cents.
The official League Ball for Junior Clubs.
Postage 5c. additional.

SPALDING'S SPECIALS FOR COMPANION READERS

SPALDING'S JUNIOR MITT.
Made of good quality soft tanned leather, well padded. Patent Lace Back and reinforced thumb.
No. CB, 25 cts.
Postage 7c. additional.
Better Quality Mitts, No. BB, 50c.; No. AB, $1; No. OXB, $2.

INFIELDERS' GLOVES.
Boys' Infielders' Glove, No. 17, 25 cents.
Better Quality Infielders' Gloves: No. XB, $1.00. 2XB, $2.00.
Postage 5c. additional.

SPALDING'S BOYS' CATCHERS' MASK.
An absolutely Safe Mask for Boys. Made of heavy wire.
No. B, $1.00.
Postage 8c. additional.
Cheaper Masks are unsafe.

SPALDING'S INFLATED BODY PROTECTOR for BOYS. No. 2, $3.50.
Postage 20c. additional.
Send for Base Ball Catalogue.

AMATEUR UNIFORMS.
Special Shirt, Pants, Cap, Belt and Stockings. Special Suit Complete, $4.80 each. Net price to clubs ordering for entire team, $3.50 per Suit. Express charges paid by the purchaser. Colors: White, Gray-Brown Mix and Dark Gray. All made by same workmen as make best League Suits.

For the past twenty-two years the Spalding Ball has been the Official Base Ball adopted and used by the National League and must be used to make the game official. Each Ball is wrapped in tin-foil, packed in a box and guaranteed to stand the test of a full game.

Spalding's Base Ball Guide, the Official Rules of the National Game, by mail, prepaid, 10c.

The Spalding Policy

One Price to All, Everywhere.

This year you can buy Spalding's Athletic Goods in the smallest towns at exactly the same price you would pay in New York or Chicago—one price everywhere. We prefer that you buy of your local dealer, but will fill orders direct when dealers do not carry our line.

Every boy who wants the latest and official information about Base Ball—the game, the regulation requirements, etc., or about any other Athletic Sports, should apply to A. G. Spalding & Bros., New York, Denver, Chicago, the Official Headquarters for all Athletic Goods.

One Standard of Quality in Athletic Goods—"The Spalding"—our exclusive trade-mark.

If your dealer doesn't sell Spalding goods, send your name and address —and his, too—on a postal, and we will send, free, our Catalogue, giving lowest retail prices on goods of our manufacture. Prices the same —no more, no less—throughout the United States.

A. G. SPALDING & BROS.

NEW YORK   DENVER   CHICAGO

Baseball History

Alexander Cartwright's rules in the 1840s were fairly well accepted, with some variations around the country. Cartwright himself did not stick around too long to see baseball develop. He left New York and headed westward to settle in Hawaii. Along the way, he introduced baseball to villages and towns across America. He was like Johnny Appleseed planting apple trees as he traveled.

In the years following that famous game at Elysian Fields, in Hoboken, many towns formed their own teams. Anyone could watch for free. The players played for no money, just for the honor of their town. The rules would be a bit different from one town to the next. People called it the "New England Game" or the "New York Game," or other names for slightly different rules.

In the 1860s, the game was so popular that two brothers, George and Harry Wright, decided that some money could be made with baseball. The Wright Brothers (*not* the same men who invented the airplane later on), moved to Cincinnati where they formed the Red Stockings, the first professional team. Professional meant that the players earned salaries for playing. People paid an admission fee to see the Red Stockings. The team traveled around America and took challenges from the best any town could offer.

The Red Stockings, who had more practice than anyone else and worked hard at being the best, were very successful. Their first season, 1869, produced 56 victories and one tie. No one could beat them. In 1870, they ran their streak to 79 games before losing to the Brooklyn Atlantics. The great winning streak made the Red Stockings famous throughout the land.

Other people saw the team's success and decided to form their own professional teams as well. The first league—a combination of teams, all salaried, playing against each other for a championship—was called the National Association. It began in 1871 and lasted five seasons.

But it was a rowdy league. Fans bet on the games and often had fights in the stands. It was thought that some players, working with gamblers, lost games on purpose. Fans would throw soda bottles at umpires or fight with them after games. Men drank liquor in the stands. Women and children wouldn't even think of going to the games. Some teams wouldn't even show up for games and wouldn't finish out their schedules.

The players themselves were rough-and-tumble men of limited education. No one really looked up to a professional ballplayer in those days.

In 1876, some decent men, who wished to provide honest and honorable baseball, met and formed the **National League,** the same National League that exists today. (One of them was Albert Spalding, who later formed a sporting goods business to supply teams with equipment.) They set forth tough rules prohibiting gambling and other forms of rowdiness. Fans were better behaved. The teams played full schedules and pennant winners were accepted by all as honest.

In 1882, another major league, the American Association, was formed. Although it didn't last too many years, it established the value of two major leagues and a World Series between them. It ended its run in 1891, but ten years later came the birth of the **American League,** and the beginning of what we call "modern baseball."

Two events off the playing field helped to make the game widely popular around the turn of the century. One was the wonderful little song "Take Me Out to the Ball Game," written in 1908 and still sung today. The other is the famous poem "Casey at the Bat," which everyone came to love. The popularity of the song and the poem helped give people a good feeling about baseball.

What follows now are some of the major events in baseball history since the modern era began.

1901 In the American League's first season, Cy Young leads all pitchers with 33 victories, and Napoleon Lajoie leads all hitters with a .422 average.

Young wound up with 511 victories, the most ever, but he also lost the most games, 313. In 1956, the award for best pitcher in each league was named the Cy Young Award. Lajoie was a lifetime .339 batter.

1903 The first modern World Series is played, with Boston, of the young American League, defeating Pittsburgh for the first world championship.

The winner of the World Series has always been called the world champion, even though, of course, it is only the champion of the United States and Canada. This is because the game was invented here and it is assumed that our players are the best in the world. Someday, we may discover that it is not necessarily so. Japanese teams, in particular, are getting better all the time, and some day a World Series may really be played against the best team of another country.

1904 Jack Chesbro of the Yankees (then called the Highlanders), wins 41 games in one season, an all-time record.

The way baseball is played today, most starting pitchers only make 30 to 35 starts a year. So it is unlikely that we will see anyone win over 40 games in one season again.

1905 The Giants' Christy Mathewson

pitches three shutouts in the World Series victory over the Philadelphia Athletics.

The fans loved Matty. He was a college-educated gentleman and one of the first players parents would encourage their children to cheer for. A more polite crowd went to the games that Christy pitched, without the rowdiness that still existed on occasion.

Christy
Mathewson

1906 The Chicago Cubs, led by their shortstop Joe Tinker, second baseman Johnny Evers, and first baseman Frank Chance, become the best team in the National League.

A newspaper poem about the ability of "Tinker to Evers to Chance" to make double plays so smoothly, made these three Cubs famous. In the future, all successful teams looked to have good "double-play combinations" to get pitchers out of trouble.

1908 Fred Merkle of the Giants forgets to touch second base and costs his team a big victory. The Giants wind up losing the pennant to the Cubs thanks to the "Merkle Boner."

Anyone can make an error, but managers get most upset over a "mental error," when a player just forgets to do the right thing. Poor "Bonehead" Merkle was not the only player to make a mental error, but he never lived it down.

1910 The Philadelphia Athletics, under Connie Mack, become the best team in the American League.

Connie Mack managed the A's for 50 years, until he was 87 years old! How did he keep from getting

Connie Mack

fired, as most managers are when their teams do badly? He also owned the team! He was also famous for never wearing a uniform—he managed in street clothes.

1912   Rube Marquard of the Giants wins 19 games in a row, a record for one season.

Marquard was called the "$10,000 Lemon" when he first joined the Giants because he wasn't as good as people expected. Sometimes it takes a little patience to give a player a chance to develop. Sometimes players go back to the minor leagues for more practice.

1914   Boston's "Miracle Braves" win the National League pennant after being in last place on July 4th.

There is nothing like the thrill of a hot pennant race in September to get the fans excited, especially if a team is coming from way behind. No team ever went from last place to first as quickly as this one.

1915   Ty Cobb steals 96 bases, a record which stands for 47 years.

During his career, Cobb was baseball's most fearsome player. He was a sensational hitter and a wreckless baserunner who sharpened his spikes and slid hard into enemy fielders. Everyone respected his talent, but he didn't have many friends, even on his own team, the Tigers.

1916   The New York Giants win 26 straight games, a record.

The Giants were managed by John McGraw, a star

Ty Cobb

third baseman of the 1890s and a stern manager who led the Giants to nine pennants in his 30 years of running the club.

1916 Grover Cleveland Alexander pitches a record 16 shutouts in one season.

Alexander went on to win 373 games and tied Mathewson for the most wins ever in the National League. Years later, an actor named Ronald Reagan played Alexander in a movie, *The Winning Team.* Reagan became the fortieth President of the United States after he changed careers and entered politics.

1919 Branch Rickey establishes the farm system for baseball.

This meant that each team would operate several minor-league clubs and use them to train players for the majors. Minor-league baseball brought enjoyment to millions of fans in cities and towns too small to support major-league teams, and the farm system led to better coaching and instruction of players. Before the farm system, minor-league teams signed their own players and tried to sell the better ones to the major leagues. Years later, Rickey brought Jackie Robinson into the major leagues. (*See* 1947.)

1919 The Chicago White Sox lose the World Series to Cincinnati. It is later discovered that eight of the players had met secretly with gamblers and discussed "throwing" the games—losing on purpose in exchange for money. They come to be known as the "Black Sox."

The Black Sox scandal rocked the baseball world, and many wondered if the game could survive. If fans thought baseball games were fixed, the sport would be destroyed. People had to believe that players always tried their best to win.

Judge Landis

1920 Judge Kenesaw Mountain Landis is named the first Commissioner of Baseball.

The stern judge banned the eight Black Sox players for life and brought trust and honesty back to baseball. He remained as commissioner for 25 years, and was followed by "Happy" Chandler, Ford Frick, William Eckert, Bowie Kuhn, and Peter Ueberroth.

1920 The spitball is outlawed. Only those pitchers who relied on that pitch were permitted to continue to throw it. The last of these men, Burleigh Grimes, retired in 1934.

The spitball was unsanitary, but was very hard to hit. The ball danced in the air. Some pitchers still try to get away with throwing it, or with scuffing or cutting the ball to make it hard to hit, but if caught, a player can be fined and thrown out of the game.

Burleigh Grimes

1920 The Yankees purchase Babe Ruth from the Red Sox.

The Babe had been a home-run slugger and a star pitcher for the Red Sox. Raised in an orphanage, he joined professional baseball at age 19, so young he was nicknamed "Babe." His real name was George Herman Ruth. On the Yankees, he became an outfielder so his bat could be in the lineup every day. And the Babe turned the home run into baseball's most exciting play. His great slugging helped save baseball from thoughts of the Black Sox, and he became the most famous player of all time. The Yankees won six pennants in the next eight years, while the Red Sox, who sold or traded all of their best players to the Yankees, went 28 years without a pennant after selling off "The Bambino," also called the "Sultan of Swat."

Babe Ruth

1920 The Dodgers and Braves play a 1–1 tie in 26 innings.

A few games each year end in ties when a local law might force a game to end by a certain hour and no team has won. All the records count, but it must be replayed from the start. Before lights were installed in ballparks, there were more ties, with darkness forcing the end of games. In this 26-inning game, both pitchers, Leon Cadore and Joe Oeschger, worked the entire game!

1920 Ray Chapman of Cleveland is hit in the head by a pitch and killed. It is the only death in major-league history on the field.

Not until the 1950s did baseball require the wearing of helmets. One wonders what took so long.

1920 Bill Wambsganss of Cleveland makes an unassisted triple play in the World Series.

Triple plays—three outs on one batted ball—only happen three or four times a season. For one player to catch the ball and get all three outs is so rare, it has only happened eight times. And Wambsganss managed to do it in a World Series!

1923 Tris Speaker leads the American League with 59 doubles, the eighth time he leads in that category.

Speaker, one of the best center fielders ever (he played very shallow and often threw runners out on the bases), batted .345 over his career and his 793 doubles is also an all-time record.

1924 Rogers Hornsby of the St. Louis Cardinals bats .424, a record for one season.

Hornsby's lifetime average of .358 was second only to Cobb. He won seven batting titles and batted over .400 three times.

1926 Hornsby is traded to the Giants for Frankie Frisch.

Rogers
Hornsby

When a big star is traded for a big star, the fans call it a blockbuster trade! Frisch, known as the "Fordham Flash" (he went right from Fordham University to the major leagues), later became manager of the wacky, colorful "Gashouse Gang" Cardinals that featured Pepper Martin, Leo Durocher, Dizzy and Daffy Dean, and Ducky Medwick.

1927 Babe Ruth belts 60 home runs in one season.

The 1927 Yankees were known as "Murderers' Row," and are considered by many to be the greatest team of all time. Ruth's teammate Lou Gehrig hit 47 homers. No other *team* in the league had more than 56 home runs that year.

1928 Ty Cobb retires with a .367 career average.

No wonder he retired! He batted "only" .323 in his last season at age 41. Cobb won 12 batting titles, had over 4,000 hits, and almost 900 stolen bases. The only time he batted less than .320 was in his rookie season.

1930 Bill Terry leads the National League with a .401 average. Hack Wilson leads the league with 56 home runs and 190 RBIs.

This was a year for hitters. Baseball has been like that—sometimes the hitters overpower the pitchers, sometimes it is a pitcher's year. Terry was the last National Leaguer to hit .400. Wilson, although only 5 feet 6 inches tall, still holds the N.L. record for home runs in one season, and his 190 RBIs is a major-league record.

1931 Lefty Grove of the Philadelphia Athletics leads the American League with 31 victories.

Grove, one of the outstanding pitchers of all time, was the last American Leaguer to win more than 30 games until 1968, when Detroit's Denny McLain won 31.

1932 Jimmie Foxx hits 58 home runs for the Athletics.

This was a close call for Ruth's record of 60, but Foxx fell short. During his career, Jimmie hit 534 home runs, which was bettered only by Ruth at the time Foxx retired.

1933 The first All-Star Game is played, in Chicago's Comiskey Park.

Each summer, the best American Leaguers have squared off against the best from the National League. Who do you think hit the first All-Star Game home run? His initials were B.R.

1934 In the second All-Star Game, the Giants' Carl Hubbell strikes out five American Leaguers in a row, all future members of the Hall of Fame—Babe Ruth, Lou Gehrig, Jimmie Foxx, Al Simmons, and Joe Cronin.

Dizzy Dean

Hubbell had a brilliant career, but he was always best remembered for these few minutes of pitching in a game that really didn't count.

1934 The Cardinals' Dizzy Dean wins 30 games.

He is the last National Leaguer to do it. Ol' Diz, one of the zaniest of the Gashouse Gang, later became a sports announcer who said such odd things as, "The runner slud into third."

1935 The first night game is played, in Cincinnati.

Walter Johnson

Eventually, all parks, except Chicago's Wrigley Field, built lights, and night games became more common than day games. But for many years they were quite a novelty.

1936 The first election is held for the Baseball Hall of Fame. Ty Cobb, Honus Wagner, Babe Ruth, Christy Mathewson, and Walter Johnson are selected.

Three years later, the Hall of Fame and Museum was opened in Cooperstown, N.Y. There are more than 200 people in the Hall of Fame today. Each year there are two elections, and those voted in, or those who fall short of election, usually get fans arguing over whether the right people made it in.

1936 The Yankees, under manager Joe McCarthy, begin a new era of domination in the American League.

Babe Ruth had retired, but Joe DiMaggio came along to team with Gehrig as the Yankee dynasty continued. The Yanks won eight pennants under McCarthy.

Honus Wagner

1936 Bob Feller breaks in with the Cleveland Indians at age 17.

Despite missing three years during military service in World War II, Feller won 266 games, pitched three no-hitters, 12 one-hitters, and led the league in strikeouts seven times. He was an Iowa farmboy who learned to pitch by throwing against the side of a barn.

Bob Feller

1937 Pie Traynor of Pittsburgh retires with a .320 lifetime average.

Traynor was generally considered the best third baseman in history until Brooks Robinson and Mike Schmidt came along many years later to challenge him for that honor. Who is the best at each position? There is no one answer. Each fan can have his own opinion.

1938 Detroit's Hank Greenberg hits 58 home runs.

Another close challenger to Ruth, but, again, he fell short.

1938 Cincinnati's Johnny Vander Meer hurls two no-hitters in a row.

There are usually only three or four no-hitters pitched a season, and some very good pitchers have never done it. Vander Meer, in pitching two in a week, did something that may never be equaled again. But every time a pitcher fires a no-hitter, everyone remembers Vander Meer and wonders if his accomplishment can be repeated.

1939 Lou Gehrig's record of playing in 2,130 consecutive games comes to an end. It represented some 14 seasons without missing a game, all for the New York Yankees.

Gehrig was known as the "Iron Horse," because he was so strong and injury-free. That made it all the more shocking that it was a rare disease—today called "Lou Gehrig's Disease"—that suddenly halted his career, and, two years later, his life. He was only 37 years old.

Lou Gehrig

1939 The first televised baseball game is played, in Ebbets Field, Brooklyn.

By the 1950s, people were tuning in baseball all over the country. Eventually, baseball on television was a way of life, as baseball on radio had been in earlier times. It is not unusual to get a worldwide TV audience of more than 80 million homes for a World Series game.

1941 Joe DiMaggio hits safely in 56 consecutive games, a record.

THE FIRST BOOK OF BASEBALL

This was his most famous and probably his most unbeatable accomplishment. DiMaggio, "The Yankee Clipper," would be voted baseball's Greatest Living Player in a poll of fans taken in 1969 (Babe Ruth was voted Greatest Ever).

1941 Ted Williams bats .406, the last batter to top .400.

Williams, "The Splendid Splinter" (because he was so thin as a young player), hit 521 career home runs, including one on his final at bat in 1960. Williams was not popular with sportswriters, to whom he was occasionally rude, and when they voted for Most Valuable Player of 1941, DiMaggio won easily.

Joe DiMaggio

1944 Joe Nuxhall, age 15, pitches for the Cincinnati Reds, the youngest player ever to appear in the major leagues.

During World War II, most players were off to military service, and the major leagues were hard pressed to keep going. Many older players returned to action. In St. Louis, the Browns even employed a one-armed outfielder named Pete Gray.

1945 The Giants' Mel Ott hits his 500th career home run.

Ott wound up with 511, which remained a National League record until Willie Mays and Henry Aaron came along. Ott had power, but was helped by very short distances down the foul lines in his home park, New York's Polo Grounds. He also had an odd batting style, raising his front foot before swinging.

Ted Williams

1945 Josh Gibson helps the Homestead Grays to their ninth consecutive Negro National League pennant.

All these years, black players had their own leagues because no major-league team would sign them. Gibson was a catcher, and the mightiest hitter of the Negro Leagues, but he never had a chance to show what he could do in the major leagues.

Josh Gibson

1946 The Braves' Warren Spahn, age 25, wins his first major-league game.

Twenty-five was old for a rookie then. Despite his late start, Spahn went on to win 363 games, including nine 20-victory seasons. He even pitched a no-hitter when he was 40, long after most players have retired. Spahn was one of many great players, like DiMaggio, Feller, Williams, and Musial, whose lifetime records would have been even better had they not gone off to serve their country during the war.

1947 Jackie Robinson signs to play with the Brooklyn Dodgers, the first black player in the major leagues in the twentieth century.

At last, the unwritten agreement among the club owners, which had kept the game all white, was over. As the first black player, Robinson had to convince people that he had not only the ability to play as well as anyone, but that he could take the loneliness and unfriendliness that went with being the first. With great dignity, he did, and opened the door for hundreds of talented black players to follow.

Jackie Robinson and Branch Rickey

1949 Casey Stengel becomes manager of the Yankees.

This opened another great Yankee era—10 pennants in 12 years, including five straight World Championships in his first five years. Stengel used a "platoon system" in managing, starting right-handed hitters against lefty pitchers and left-handed hitters against righty pitchers, which gave the batters an edge. Casey was also a colorful character whose doubletalk was called "Stengelese."

Casey Stengel

1951 Bobby Thomson's home run wins the pennant for the New York Giants against the Brooklyn Dodgers in a playoff game.

The Dodgers and Giants, playing in the same city, were arch rivals, and they ended the season tied for first. To decide the champion, they played a three-game playoff, and Thomson's homer, in the last of the ninth of the final game, has become perhaps the most famous in baseball history.

1951 Joe DiMaggio retires. Willie Mays and Mickey Mantle enter the major leagues.

As old stars leave, new ones always seem to come along. Mantle moved right into DiMaggio's centerfield spot for the Yankees and went on to hit 536 home runs as the most powerful switch-hitter in history. Mays could "do it all," starring for the Giants at bat, in the field, and on the bases. He would hit 660 home runs.

1952 Ralph Kiner wins his seventh home-run title in a row.

Willie Mays

Kiner played for Pittsburgh at a time when they weren't very good. But sometimes, even bad teams can have exciting players, and Kiner was that, giving Pirate fans something to cheer about every day.

1952 Relief pitcher Hoyt Wilhelm homers in his first time at bat in the major leagues.

Homering in a first at bat is a rarity, but Wilhelm went on to pitch in 1,070 games—the most ever—and never hit another home run! His baffling knuckleball made him a relief star well into his forties, and he was the first relief pitcher elected to the Hall of Fame.

1953 The Boston Braves move to Milwaukee.

This began a series of shifts of teams, all of which had stayed in place for half a century. The Athletics moved from Philadelphia to Kansas City (and later to Oakland), the Browns moved from St. Louis to Baltimore and became the Orioles, and, in 1958, the Brooklyn Dodgers moved to Los Angeles and the New York Giants to San Francisco, expanding the major leagues to the West Coast. The Braves moved again, in 1966, to Atlanta, and were later replaced in Milwaukee by the Brewers.

Roy Campanella

1955 Roy Campanella wins his third Most Valuable Player Award and the Dodgers win their only world championship in Brooklyn.

The long-suffering fans of the "Brooklyn Bums" finally beat the Yankees in their sixth World Series meeting. Campy, with Duke Snider, Pee Wee Reese, Jackie Robinson, Gil Hodges, and Carl Furillo, came to be known as the "Boys of Summer." Roy never made it to Los Angeles with the Dodgers, as an auto accident in 1958 left him in a wheelchair for the rest of his life.

1956 The Yankees' Don Larsen pitches a perfect game in the World Series.

A perfect game is very rare, better than a no-hitter. In a no-hitter, there can be walks and errors. In a perfect game, no one reaches base at all. Very few of these games have been pitched, and Larsen (normally a rather ordinary pitcher) did this during the World Series! Considering all the attention, many think of this as the greatest game ever pitched.

Catcher Yogi Berra congratulates Don Larsen

1958 Ernie Banks hits 47 home runs, a record for shortstops.

The Chicago Cubs infielder was called "Mr. Cub" and always had a smile and a sunny disposition. Like Kiner in Pittsburgh, Banks was the bright spot on a losing team. He was the first National Leaguer to win two Most Valuable Player Awards in a row.

1961 After nearly 60 years of both the American and National Leagues having eight teams each, the leagues expand to 10 each (the A.L. in 1961, the N.L. in 1962). In 1969 they increase to 12 each, and the A.L. adds two more in 1977.

The new teams were called expansion teams. The best known was the New York Mets—in 1962 they

Mickey Mantle

Roger Maris

lost 120 games, a record, but in 1969 they amazed the sports world by winning the World Series when everyone thought they would finish last as usual. Expansion also increased the schedule from 154 to 162 games.

1961 Roger Maris breaks Babe Ruth's record by hitting 61 home runs in one season.

The most exciting home-run race in history, as Maris and roommate Mickey Mantle battled to break Ruth's record *and* beat each other. Mantle wound up with 54, but Maris homered in his last game of the season to bring down the most famous baseball record. There was such pressure on Roger from newspapers, radio, and television, that his hair began to fall out. Adding drama to this chase was Commissioner Ford Frick's ruling that unless Ruth's record was broken in 154 games, both Babe's mark and the new mark would be listed.

1961 Whitey Ford breaks Babe Ruth's pitching record by hurling 33⅔ consecutive innings without allowing a run in World Series competition.

1961 was not a big year for the Babe. Two of his best records fell, this one dating back to his days as a Red Sox pitcher. Ford also holds the record for wins in World Series history, with 10 games.

1962 The Dodgers' Maury Wills steals 104 bases to break Ty Cobb's record of 96.

This opened a new era in which base stealing became popular, and many baseball players combined speed and power, something unheard of in earlier times. In coming years, first Lou Brock, and then Rickey Henderson, would pass Wills's record. As an example, in 1950 there were 650 stolen bases in the major leagues. In 1986, there were 3,312.

1963 Stan Musial retires with a .331 batting average and seven batting titles.

The Cardinals' great star and Ted Williams were the best hitters of the 1940s and 1950s. Musial was so popular that when he retired, they built a statue of him outside Busch Stadium in St. Louis.

1963 Yogi Berra plays in his last World Series, his record 14th.

Stan Musial

Yogi was a funny-looking catcher who said things like, "It ain't over 'til it's over," but he was a genius on the baseball field and success seemed to follow him. As a player, coach, and manager, he was in 22 World Series.

1965 Houston's Astrodome opens, baseball's first indoor field.

The problem with a park with a roof was that the grass wouldn't grow. This led to the quick invention of "Astroturf," an artificial playing surface later used in many outdoor parks as well. Artificial surfaces produce higher bounces and fewer bad hops, but also faster grounders that infielders have trouble getting to when not hit close to them.

Yogi Berra

1965 Bert Campaneris plays all nine positions in a nine-inning game.

Campaneris, normally the Athletics' shortstop,

spent one inning at each position, even pitcher. Three years later, Minnesota's Cesar Tovar also played nine positions in one game. Although in school a good athlete is usually able to play any position, by the time he reaches the majors a player is most at home at one position. What Campaneris and Tovar did was strictly a gimmick to draw fans.

1965 Satchel Paige pitches three innings for Kansas City at age 59.

Paige was the greatest pitcher in the Negro Leagues, but never got to pitch in the majors in his prime. He finally had his chance in 1951, but fans missed seeing him at his best. This appearance for the Athletics was his last in the majors, although another one-time-only gimmick by the A's. Satch's best years were with the Pittsburgh Crawfords and Kansas City Monarchs of the Negro Leagues in the 1930s and 1940s.

Satchel Paige

1966 Frank Robinson becomes the first player to win the Most Valuable Player Award in both leagues, having won in 1961 in the N.L. and 1966 in the A.L.

Robinson went on to hit 586 career home runs, third on the all-time list. In 1975, while still playing, he became the major's first black manager. Playing managers are no longer common, but in the 1920s and 1930s many teams had playing managers, especially because it saved them having to pay a manager's salary during the nation's Great Depression, when money was hard to come by.

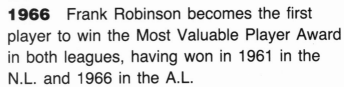

THE FIRST BOOK OF BASEBALL

1966 Sandy Koufax earns his fifth consecutive earned-run-average title, his third Cy
Young Award, and wins a career-high 27
games.

After this season, fearing permanant damage to his
arm, he retired. He had four no-hitters and a host of
strikeout records, and was considered the best pitcher of the 1960s. But his doctor told him he could
damage his arm if he kept pitching. Koufax retired
while he was still at his best, but today, doctors
know how to correct his problem with arthroscopic
surgery.

1967 Boston, which had finished ninth in
1966, rallied to win one of the tightest pennant races of all time.

With Carl Yastrzemski winning the Triple Crown,
this great Boston triumph was known as the "Impossible Dream." In the final weekend of the season, four teams—Boston, Minnesota, Detroit, and
Chicago—all still had a chance to win the pennant.

1968 Bob Gibson has a 1.12 earned run
average and shuts out every opponent except
the Dodgers at least once.

This was the Year of the Pitcher, and Gibson was
the best of the lot. Detroit's Denny McLain won 31
games, and the Dodgers' Don Drysdale hurled six
shutouts in a row. Hitters had such a tough time that
only one batter in the American League hit over
.300. The next year, the pitching mound was low-
ered. Gibson, who was overpowering, won seven

Sandy Koufax

Bob Gibson

games in nine World Series starts over his career, with a 1.89 earned run average for the Cardinals.

1969 Baseball expands to Canada with the addition of the Montreal Expos.

The American League added the Toronto Blue Jays in 1977 to give each league a Canadian team. The 1969 expansion also created the League Championship Series, so that each league had eastern and western divisions, the champions of which would meet after the regular season—with the winners going on to the World Series.

1972 Players go on strike for the first time. The start of the season was delayed a week as the players union ordered a strike against the teams to improve pensions for retired players.

1972 Roberto Clemente, flying emergency supplies to earthquake victims in Nicaragua on New Year's Eve, is lost at sea when his plane crashes. He was only 38 years old.

Roberto Clemente

Clemente was the greatest of the Latin American stars, a four-time batting champion who had 3,000 hits and was a sensational outfielder. He was also a man of great courage as his final act proved.

1973 The American League begins the designated-hitter rule, the biggest rule change of the century. Instead of the pitcher batting (usually a weak hitter), a "DH" could take his place in the batting order, and the pitcher could remain in the game.

The National League did not accept this rule, creating a major difference between the two leagues. Most colleges, minor leagues, and amateur leagues did accept it. Why are pitchers such poor hitters? Most spend so much time practicing their pitching they cannot worry about batting practice. And even the best hitters need frequent practice to keep in top form.

1974 Mike Marshall of the Dodgers pitches in 106 games.

No pitcher had ever worked that often. Besides the DH rule and the increase in stolen bases, the use of relief pitchers has been the biggest change in today's baseball. No successful team can be without a good relief ace. It is no longer considered important for pitchers to pitch complete games. A relief pitcher who holds on to a lead for his team is given credit for a "save."

1974 Hank Aaron breaks Babe Ruth's career home-run record of 714.

For many years, people thought Ruth's record would stand forever. But Aaron kept plugging away, hitting about forty homers a year even as he got older. Suddenly, fans realized he was going to catch Ruth after all. And with his first two swings of 1974, Aaron tied and then broke the record. He wound up with 755 career home runs, and again, people think Aaron's record will stand forever.

1975 Catfish Hunter becomes baseball's first millionaire player.

After winning the Cy Young Award for 1975, Hun-

Hank Aaron

ter's salary wasn't paid on time, and he was declared a "free agent," eligible to sign a new contract with anyone. The Yankees signed him for five years. Up until this time, most players had only one-year contracts, but the "reserve clause" kept them with their teams even after the contracts ran out.

1975 Rennie Stennett of the Pirates gets seven hits in a nine-inning game.

This tied the record set in 1892 by Wilbert Robinson. Getting seven times at bat in nine innings is tough enough—seven hits is amazing!

1976 Andy Messersmith and Dave McNally refuse to sign their one-year contracts and win their test of the reserve clause.

Baseball bargained a new agreement under which players were now reserved for only six years, rather than for their entire careers. After six years, they could become free agents and choose to find a new team. Teams began paying much higher salaries for free agents, or to keep their own players from becoming free agents.

Reggie Jackson

1977 Reggie Jackson of the Yankees belts five home runs in the World Series, including three in one game, and four on four consecutive swings over two games. It is the most explosive World-Series performance ever.

Reggie was a winner, first with Oakland, then with the Yankees. He was known as "Mr. October" for his clutch hitting in big games. Although he struck out more than any player in history and batted .300 only once, he was probably the most exciting player of his time and, like Ruth, great fun to watch whether he was striking out or belting a long homer.

1981 The players strike for seven weeks.

This was the summer of no baseball, the saddest baseball season. The players thought the owners were trying to stop their free-agency rights. Everyone was a loser on this strike, especially the fans.

1981 Nolan Ryan pitches the fifth no-hitter of his career.

The great fastballer would also set the record for most strikeouts in one season (383) and in a career, breaking Walter Johnson's record and passing the 4,000 mark.

1982 Paul Molitor of the Milwaukee Brewers gets five hits in a World Series game.

Five hits in a game is unusual, but it still happens about a dozen times a season. But not until this year, the 79th year of the World Series, did a player finally do it in a World Series game.

Pete Rose

1985 Pete Rose gets his 4,193rd hit to break Ty Cobb's record.

Pete was just a hard-working, scrappy player who gave it his all. He wasn't blessed with natural ability, he had to work for everything he got. He didn't run fast, didn't have much power, wasn't a great defensive player, but he was a winner. He broke a lot of records, but this was his biggest.

Tom Seaver

1986 Tom Seaver pitches his 16th opening-day game.

It is an honor to be chosen to pitch on opening day. Usually, the "ace" of the pitching staff gets the assignment. No one was handed the ball more often on opening day than Seaver, the first great star of the Mets, and one of the best pitchers of his time.

1986 Roger Clemens strikes out 20 batters in one game.

This was a record for a nine-inning game, and one can only wonder if, some day, someone will come along who can get 27 strikeouts in one game—three each inning.

1987 Rookie records are set by Mark McGwire of Oakland (49 home runs) and Benito Santiago of San Diego (34 game hitting streak); Don Mattingly sets the record with six grand-slam homers, and ties another by belting homers in eight consecutive games for the Yankees.

This was a big year for sluggers and not a very good one for pitchers. Some said the ball may have been manufactured "livelier," but baseball officials denied it. In one game, the Toronto Blue Jays set a record with ten home runs.

Figuring It Out:

MATH, BASEBALL STATISTICS, AND KEEPING SCORE

You can follow your favorite player or team by checking the newspapers each day, which are loaded with information on the major leagues.

You can see the standings of the clubs, the box scores of games, and the league leaders in many categories. You can often see a chart showing how everyone on the home team is hitting or pitching.

It is good to know how all of these baseball averages are figured. You can do it yourself with the help of a calculator.

Batting Averages. A batting average measures how many hits a player would get if he were to bat 1000 times. Anything over .300 is considered excellent.

Use the division sign for the word *for*. If a batter has 71 hits *for* 253 at bats, you would calculate 71 ÷ 253 = .2806324. Since batting averages are only shown in three numbers, you would round off the third number and this average would be .281. If the fourth number is five or more, add a number in the third column.

Try another one. Look at the league leaders and see if the math is correct!

Slugging percentage. This statistic uses total bases to determine how powerful the hitter is. A single is one base, a double two, a triple three, and a home run four. If a player hits one of each of those, he has 10 total bases $(1 + 2 + 3 + 4 = 10)$. If he has done it in 10 official at bats, 10 total bases *for* 10 at bats is a slugging percentage of 1.000. You can have a slugging percentage of more than 1.000, because you can have as many as four total bases for every at bat—if you hit a home run every time up.

Won–Lost Percentage and Games Behind in the Standings. Standings are based on won–lost percentage. To figure a won–lost percentage, first you have to add up the wins and losses to see how many games a team has played. Let's say they have 43 wins and 38 losses. $43 + 38 = 81$. Remember that number—81—and clear the calculator.

Now think of the division sign as the word *for* again. This team is 43 for 81, or $43 \div 81 = .5308641$. Round that off just like a batting average and the team is at .531.

Check the standings in the newspapers. Are they correct for your favorite teams?

You can use this same method to figure out a pitcher's won–lost percentage.

The standings also tell you how many games behind the first place team everyone is. Figuring out the games-behind column can be tricky. You count up the difference in wins and loses between the two teams and divide that difference by two.

For example:

	W	L	GB
New York	47	31	—
Chicago	44	32	2

New York has three more wins and one less defeat than Chicago. Adding three and one gives you four, and dividing four by two gives you two. Chicago is two games behind in this example.

When one team has played an even number of games and the other an odd number, differences of half games result in the games behind. By the end of the year, everyone should have played the same number of games, so it should all even out by then.

Earned Run Average. This is a very important statistic for pitchers. **The number tells you how many earned runs they allow for every nine innings they pitch.** An earned run is a run that scores without help from errors, even a pitcher's own error. It is a run that has scored simply by hits, walks, and hit batters.

Clear the calculator. Punch in the earned runs (say, 60) and multiply it by 9.60 × 9 = 540. Leave the 540 showing. Don't clear the calculator. Hit the ÷ sign, and then punch in the innings pitched, say 210. That gives you an ERA of 2.5714285, which rounds off to 2.57. This is a good pitcher, one who allows fewer than three runs for every nine innings.

Fielding Percentage. This is a stat for fielders. You divide the total number of assists and putouts a fielder has made by the total number of assists, putouts, *and* errors. If a fielder has made 108 putouts, 14 assists, and 2 errors, you divide 122 (108 + 14 = 122) by 124 (108 + 14 + 2 = 124). This fielder has a .984 fielding percentage out of a possible 1.000.

KEEPING SCORE

Statistics in baseball come from people who keep score during the games. Keeping score doesn't just mean knowing how many runs are on the scoreboard. It means keeping track of every play during the game.

Use this system of symbols in each batter's individual box on the scorecard to indicate how he was retired or reached base.

Fielding plays retiring batters or runners call for the use of the number symbols. For example, the batter who grounds out to the third baseman is retired 5-3. If he flied to the leftfielder, you use the number 7.

The lower left-hand corner of the scoring block should be considered as home plate. Progress is made counter-clockwise with progress to first base indicated in lower right-hand corner; to second in upper right-hand corner; to third in upper left-hand corner; and to home in lower left. It is convenient to encircle all runs so that scoring plays may be seen at a glance.

Number Players as Follows:

1—Pitcher; 2—Catcher; 3—First Baseman; 4—Second Baseman; 5—Third Baseman; 6—Shortstop; 7—Leftfielder; 8—Centerfielder; 9—Rightfielder.

Symbols for Plays

—	Single	BK	Balk
=	Double	K	Strike Out
≡	Triple	BB	Base on Balls
▬	Home Run	FO	Force Out
E	Reached base on error	SF	Sacrifice Fly
FC	Fielder's Choice	DP	Double Play
HP	Hit By Pitcher	F	Foul Fly
WP	Wild Pitch	IW	Intentional Walk
SB	Stolen Base	L	Line Drive
SH	Sacrifice Hit	B	Bunt
PB	Passed Ball		

Scorecard (INNING 1)

No		Pos	1	2	
	2ND BASE	4			4 singled, thrown out stealing (catcher to shortstop)
	CENTERFIELD	8			8 doubled, advanced to 3rd on a fielder's choice, scored on passed ball
	3RD BASE	5			5 thrown out (2nd to 1st)—fielder's choice.
	SHORTSTOP	6			6 hit by pitcher, took 1st base
	1ST BASE	3			3 flied out to center field—end of inning
					INNING 2
	CATCHER	2			2 walked, later forced out shortstop to 2nd base (1st half of double play)
	LEFT FIELD	7			7 hit into double play (shortstop to 2nd base to 1st base)
	RIGHT FIELD	9			9 hit home run
	PITCHER	1			1 fouled out to 1st base
Totals					

An example of a score card.

Most ballparks sell score sheets. The next time you go to a game, you might have fun keeping score.

There are complex systems and simple systems. Here's a simple system.

Each position is given a number. 1—Pitcher, 2—Catcher, 3—First Baseman, 4—Second Baseman, 5—Third Baseman, 6—Shortstop, 7—Left Fielder, 8—Center Fielder, 9—Right Fielder, DH—Designated Hitter.

Plays are represented by symbols. A single is one line −. A double is two =. A triple is three ≡. And a home run is four ≣.

Here's a list of other handy symbols.
Walk—BB (an intentional walk is IBB), Sacrifice Hit—SH, Sacrifice Fly—SF, Strikeout—SO or K (some people use K for a strikeout swinging and KC for a called third strike), Balk—BK, Foul Fly—F, Fielder's Choice—FC, Hit by Pitch—HP, Wild Pitch—WP, Passed Ball—PB, Stolen Base—SB, Force Out—FO, Double Play—DP, and Error—E.

You use these numbers and symbols to show what every batter did when he came to the plate.

For instance, if the batter hit a grounder to the shortstop who threw to first for the out, it would be scored 6–3. If he hit a sacrifice fly to right field, it would be scored 9SF.

The Grand Old Game Keeps Rolling

JOSEPH PAUL DI MAGGIO
NEW YORK A.L. 1936 TO 1951

HIT SAFELY IN 56 CONSECUTIVE GAMES
FOR MAJOR LEAGUE RECORD 1941. HIT 2
HOME-RUNS IN ONE INNING 1936. HIT 3
HOME-RUNS IN ONE GAME (3 TIMES). HOLDS
NUMEROUS BATTING RECORDS. PLAYED IN
10 WORLD SERIES (51 GAMES) AND 11 ALL
STAR GAMES. MOST VALUABLE PLAYER
A.L. 1939, 1941, 1947.

Joe DiMaggio's plaque
at the Hall of Fame.

One of the joys of being a baseball fan is seeing new and exciting players entering the major leagues every year. The flow has never stopped. As Ruth and Cobb retired, on came DiMaggio and Musial. With their aging and retirement came Mantle and Mays.

Today's baseball has been gifted with athletes who seem to put power and speed together as no generation has in the past. Are today's players better than the old-timers? It is always hard to compare. Their records aren't always better, but that might just mean that the pitching is better, and it makes hitting tougher. Surely, hard-throwing relief pitchers make hitting tougher than ever. And equipment is better today. New balls are always used. In olden times, they would try to play a whole game with one dead ball.

VRJC LIBRARY

In sports like track and field or swimming, where everything is measured by the clock, today's athletes easily surpass all the old records. If that is so, why can't we also believe that baseball players are also better? It may well be the case.

Today's stars could play at any time, against any opponents. Just calling off their names makes you anxious to be in Cooperstown when their time comes for the Hall of Fame: Rickey Henderson, Eric Davis, Andre Dawson, Don Mattingly, Dwight Gooden, Kirby Puckett, Ron Guidry, Wade Boggs, Darryl Strawberry, Ozzie Smith, Dale Murphy, Pedro Guerrero, Robin Yount, Eddie Murray, Cal Ripken, Vince Coleman, Gary Carter, Mike Scott, Jim Rice, Wally Joyner, Tony Gwynn, George Bell, Keith Hernandez, Tim Raines, Fernando Valenzuela, George Brett, Ryne Sandberg, Dave Parker, Dave Winfield, Alan Trammell . . . Wow!

> *Take me out to the ballgame,*
> *Take me out to the crowd . . .*
> *Buy me some peanuts and Cracker Jack*
> *I don't care if I never get back*
> *For it's root, root, root*
> *for the home team*
> *If they don't win it's a shame*
> *For it's one . . . two . . .*
> *three strikes you're out*
> *At the old, ball game!*

Glossary

SOME BASEBALL WORDS AND TERMS

(common abbreviations are in parentheses)

Around the horn   The term for throwing the baseball from third to second to first. Used to describe a double play of that sort, or what infielders do after an out if no one is on base (although they let the shortstop participate, too).

Assist (A)   Credit given to a fielder who has helped get an opposing player out, usually with a throw.

At bats (AB)   The number of times a batter has been at bat. This number does not include Walks, Hit by Pitch, Sacrifices, or Catcher's Interference.

Avg.   Abbreviation for average. By itself, Avg. usually means Batting Average (see below).

Bad hop   A tricky bounce, often caused by hitting a pebble in the infield, or a seam on artificial grass.

Balk (BK)   There are many ways that a pitcher can balk. If he puts his pitching hand to his mouth while standing on the rubber—it's a balk. It counts as a ball against the batter. Other ways a pitcher can balk include: starting his delivery and then stopping, trying a pick-off without stepping toward the base, making pitching motions without having the ball in his hand, pitching without one foot on the rubber, and letting the ball drop out of his hand while his foot is on the rubber. When a balk is called, all baserunners advance one base.

Ball   A pitch outside the strike zone.

Base hit   A hit in which a batter reaches first base safely, not because of a fielder's error or fielder's choice. (See also "extra base hit.")

Bases on balls (BB)   If the pitcher throws four pitches outside the strike zone (four balls), the batter takes first base. This is also known as a walk.

Batter's box   The area defined by chalk lines around home plate in which a batter must stand. To step out of the batter's box, a batter must request time out.

Battery   The pitcher and catcher.

Batting average   (**Avg.,** also sometimes **Pct.**) A batter's statistic. It is a measure of how often he gets a hit, not on base (Walks, for instance, don't count as an official time at bat and are not included in calculating a batting average), per times at bat. A batter with a .333 batting average gets a hit once for every three at bats. The calculation of a batting average is explained on page 67.

Beanball   A duster or a brushback pitch, but usually used to describe a pitch thrown at the batter's head. Pitchers use it to keep the batter from crowding and digging in at the plate, or to get even for a home run or another close pitch. It sometimes causes fights, getting thrown out of the game by the umpire, and a fine.

Bullpen   The place where the relief pitchers watch the game, and wait for a call from the manager to relieve another pitcher. If the call comes, the bullpen is also where the relief pitcher warms up with a reserve catcher or coach. The term bullpen is also often used to describe a team's relief pitchers. "Boy, our bullpen is getting clobbered" is often a fan's lament.

Bunt   In a squared off stance, a batter bunts by softly hitting the ball in the infield.

Bush   Used to describe a minor-league action, although it is rather insulting to a minor leaguer. A "bush play" might be stealing a base when your team is winning by ten runs, when it's hardly necessary.

Called game   A game that, for any reason, is stopped by the umpires. If a game is interrupted by rain before the fifth inning, it does not count as an official game. All statistics (such as home runs and strikeouts) are erased, and the game is usually played again (starting at the first inning) at a later date in the season.

Caught looking Term used to describe taking a third strike without swinging at it.

Checked swing A half swing. It's not a strike unless the pitch is in the strike zone.

Clean-up hitter The fourth batter in the lineup. He tends to come to bat with men in scoring position more often than anyone, and has a chance to "clean up" the bases by driving runners home.

Coach Assistant to the manager. A hitting coach works with the batters, a pitching coach with the pitchers. A bullpen coach works with the relief staff and utility players. The first base coach warns baserunners about pick-offs. The third base coach signals a runner to keep going or hold up at a base, and passes signals to the batter from the manager.

Coach's box Chalked rectangles behind first and third base in which the coaches stand.

Complete game (CG) This is a pitcher's stat. It means that he pitched the entire game. A complete game can be particularly important when the bullpen needs a rest.

Count The number of balls and strikes on a batter. Balls are always given first. "One and one" means one ball and a strike.

Cut-off An infielder is often the cut-off man. He takes (or "cuts-off") a throw (usually from the outfield) and relays it to another fielder.

Cycle When a batter gets a single, double, triple, and home run in the same game, it is known as hitting for the cycle.

Double (2B) A two-base hit.

Doubleheader Two games played by the same teams on the same day.

Double play (DP) A play in which two outs are made. The most common double play happens in the infield. When a runner is on first, and the batter hits the ball between second and third, the shortstop spears the ball, flips it to the second baseman who steps on second for the force-out. Then the second baseman throws to the first baseman for the second force-out. Nothing can stop a rally faster than a double play.

Earned run average (ERA) A pitcher's stat. It is (on average) the number of earned runs a pitcher allows during a nine-inning game. Runs which score due to errors, or passed balls do not count as earned runs. The calculation for an ERA is explained on page 69.

Error (E)   A misplay by a fielder.

Extra base hit   A double, triple, or home run.

Fair territory   The playing field within the foul lines. A fair ball is a ball hit inside the foul lines, in fair territory.

Fan   1. A slang word for striking out. 2. A fan is also someone who is crazy about a sport. Fan is short for fanatic.

Fielder's choice (FC)   A play in which a fielder makes a choice between possible outs. Often a fielder will try to get the lead runner out rather than making the play at first base.

Firemen   Relief pitchers.

Force-out   See page 18.

Forfeited game   If a team has violated the rules, the umpire may call it a forfeit. The opposing side wins, and the score for any forfeited game is declared as 9–0. This very rarely occurs.

Foul territory   The area outside the foul lines. A foul ball is a ball hit outside the foul lines. A foul pole is a pole in the outfield stands that is used to judge whether a home run is a fair ball. A foul tip is a foul that comes straight back toward the catcher.

Games (G)   Used in statistics to indicate the number of games a player has appeared in.

Games pitched (G) and **Games started (GS)**   These are both stats for pitchers. **Games pitched** is the number of games in which he has pitched. **Games started** is the number of games in which he was the starting pitcher.

Grand slam   A home run with the bases loaded.

Green light   A signal from the third base coach that it is okay to swing at the next pitch. With three balls and no strikes, batters usually "take" the next pitch, hoping for a walk, unless they get the green light.

Hit-and-run   Usually a play intended to move a runner from first base to third. The baserunner runs with the pitch and as the second baseman or shortstop runs to cover the bag (thus creating a hole in the defense), the batter hits the ball in the gap. With a good head start, the runner can get to third. The

---

play requires a very skilled batter, and a good baserunner.

Hit by pitch (HBP)   A stat indicating that a batter was hit by a pitched ball.

Hits (H)   A batter's stat that records the number of times he has hit safely.

Hole   Any gap between fielders.

Home run (HR)   Usually a ball hit out of play, over the outfield fence. The batter trots around the bases from first to home since no play on him is possible. He scores a run, and any baserunners also score. With great speed, a batter can sometimes hit an inside-the-park home run.

Hot stove league   A term for a gathering of fans to discuss baseball during the winter off-season.

Infield fly rule   This is a rule that keeps fielders from dropping fly balls on purpose to get double plays or force-outs. With fewer than two outs, with runners on first and second or the bases loaded, the umpire uses his judgment to call an automatic out on a catchable pop-up. Even if it is dropped, the batter is out.

Innings pitched (IP)   A pitcher's stat indicating the number of innings pitched. Each out is a third of an inning. If the starting pitcher gets one out in the second inning and is replaced, he has pitched 1⅓ innings.

Intentional walk (IBB or **IP** for **Intentional pass)**   Four straight pitches are thrown outside the strike zone (the catcher often stands) that walk a batter intentionally. Often this is done to put a runner on first base and to try for a double play, or to avoid a power hitter.

Line drive   A well-hit ball that travels on a straight line.

Manager   The person in charge of a team during a game. He makes many crucial decisions during a game (such as signaling for a play, pinch hitting for a batter, calling for a relief pitcher, setting the lineup, etc.), and is often held responsible for a team's win or loss.

Mound   The pitcher's mound.

No-hitter   A hitless game. A pitcher has to pitch the complete game and not allow a base hit to be credited with a no-hitter. See also "perfect game."

On-base percentage   This tells you how often a player gets on base, including walks and times hit by pitch.

Passed ball A pitch that a catcher should have caught, but that got by him. See also "wild pitch."

Payoff pitch The pitch delivered with the count three balls and two strikes. Three and two is also called "full count."

Pct. An abbreviation for percentage, and the meaning can vary depending on the context.

Perfect game An extremely rare game in which there are no baserunners. A pitcher can pitch a no-hitter and still have baserunners through walks, errors, or by hitting a batter.

Pick-off Baserunners take leads off their bases. A pitcher tries to pick them off by throwing to the baseman, and the runners must be tagged.

Pinch-hitter and **pinch-runner** These are players that substitute for a batter or a baserunner to gain an edge on offense. The replaced player can't return to the game.

Putout (PO) Credited to a fielder, this means that the player made (or "put") an opposing player out.

Rally Teams rally when they're scoring runs, or even threatening to score runs.

Relief pitchers Pitchers who relieve another pitcher when he's in trouble or is tiring. There are middle relievers (who might routinely pitch the 6th and 7th innings) and short relievers (who usually come in during the 8th or 9th). A strong relief pitcher who can be counted on to "put away a game" (protect the lead) is often called the team's "stopper."

Rookie A baseball player in his first full season.

Rubber The pitcher's plate. A twenty-four-inch-long and six-inch-wide white slab positioned on the pitcher's mound. The pitcher must keep one foot on the rubber while delivering a pitch. If not, he's balked.

Run batted in (RBI) A run that scores as a direct result of a hit or sacrifice. On a "grand slam," the batter is credited with four RBIs and one run scored.

Run down When a baserunner is trapped between two bases, the fielders try to run him down and tag him out.

Run scored (R) Crossing home plate safely. Since the object of the game is to score runs, a player with many RBIs and runs scored may be more valuable to a team than a player with a higher batting average.

Sacrifice See page 29.

Saves (S or SV)   A credit that goes to a relief pitcher for preserving another pitcher's lead.

Shoestring catch   A fly ball, usually fielded by an outfielder, that is caught near the ground. If the fielder gets it on a short hop, it is said that he "trapped" the ball.

Shutouts (ShO)   Credited to a pitcher, a shutout is when an opposing team doesn't score a run.

Single (1B)   A one-base hit.

Slugging percentage (SLG)   A batter's stat, explained in full on page 68.

Stolen base (SB)   When a runner advances to the next base on his own (without a base hit by a teammate), the base is stolen. If the other team gets him out, he's caught stealing (CS).

Stopper   See "relief pitcher."

Strikeout (SO)   Three pitches in the strike zone that the batter doesn't hit are a strikeout. Some scorers use the abbreviation "K" when the batter strikes out. On a strikeout, the catcher is credited with a putout, unless he drops the third strike.

Strike zone   The area over home plate that defines balls and strikes.

Triple (3B)   A three-base hit.

Tweener   A ball hit between two outfielders, usually resulting in an extra base hit.

Umpire   An official who makes calls such as balls and strikes, whether a ball is fair or foul, and whether a baserunner is safe or out.

Utility players   A player who can play more than one position. Often a utility player is a reserve, or is filling in for an injured regular. Also sometimes called "scrubs" or "scrubeenies."

Walk (BB)   Same as a base on balls (see above).

Wild pitch (WP)   A pitch that goes by the catcher, and that the catcher could not have caught. See also "passed ball."

A Digest of Baseball Rules

A baseball game is played between two teams. Each team has nine starting players. One team plays defense in the field while the opposing team bats at home plate.

The game is played on a diamond-shaped field.

Home plate is a five-sided piece of white rubber with a flat end and a pointy end. It is seventeen inches

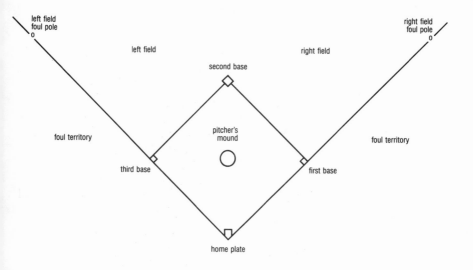

center field

left field
foul pole

right field
foul pole

left field

right field

second base

foul territory

pitcher's
mound

foul territory

third base

first base

home plate

wide and twenty-three inches long. The flat end is placed toward the pitcher, and the pitcher stands on a ten-inch-high **mound,** sixty and a half feet from home plate.

The pointed end of home plate is very important because it marks the beginning of **fair territory.** From that point, two **foul lines** are chalked that lead to first base and to third, continue into the outfield and stop at what is called a **foul pole.** The line itself, the foul pole, and inside the lines is **fair territory.** Outside the lines is **foul territory.**

If a batted ball
- stops in fair territory
- lands in fair territory and rolls foul *beyond* first or third base

it's called a **fair ball.** On a fair ball, the batter can run for a base.

If a batted ball
- stops in foul territory (without touching fair territory *beyond* first or third base)
- lands in fair territory and rolls foul *before* it passes first or third base

it's a **foul ball.** The batter can't run for a base on a foul ball, but if a fielder catches a foul ball before it hits the ground or a wall, the batter will be out.

The **bases** (sometimes also called **bags**) are white canvas, ten inches by ten, and are ninety feet apart.

HOW A BATTER CAN GET ON BASE

He can get a hit. That doesn't mean just hitting the ball. It means hitting it so that he reaches a base safely.

The batter is allowed to run *past* first base, on the first base line, after touching the base safely. He must, though, return to the base immediately.

If he overruns second or third, he can be tagged out trying to get back, but not if he overruns first base.

He can get a walk (a base on balls).

He can be hit with a pitch.

He can reach base on a fielder's error.

He can reach base on a fielder's choice.

He can also reach base in some less common ways. If he hits a ball that touches a teammate on base (and the ball wasn't deflected *off* a fielder), the teammate is out, but the batter is awarded a single. He can *try* to get to first base if the catcher doesn't catch a third strike (this is called a **dropped third strike**). On a dropped third strike, the ball is in play (just as if it were hit) and the batter must then either be tagged or thrown out at first to be put out.

THE FIRST BOOK OF BASEBALL

HOW A BATTER CAN MAKE AN OUT

He can strike out. Three strikes and down you go.

He can hit a ball that is caught. Any ball that is caught by a fielder before it hits the ground or a wall puts the batter out. Any **foul ball** that is caught can put the batter out, but a caught foul tip only counts as a strike.

He can ground out. This is a ball hit on the ground (a **grounder**), usually to an infielder, who scoops it up and throws to first before the batter gets there.

He can sacrifice. When a ball is dead, a runner may advance *if the rules say he can, and no play on the runner can be made.*

The ball is dead when
- The batter is hit by a pitch. Runners advance a base *only if* they're **forced.** Since only one runner can be on a base, sometimes an incoming teammate "forces" a runner off a base and on to the next one.
- The ball goes foul. Runners can't advance.
- A pitch hits a baserunner trying to score. Runners advance one base.
- The umpire calls "time out" for any reason (including a manager or player's request). Runners can't advance.
- A fielder falls into the seats or dugout while making a catch. Runners advance one base.
- A fielder throws the ball into the seats or dugout, out of play. Runners advance two bases. But baserunners can make outs, too.

HOW A BASERUNNER CAN MAKE AN OUT
He can be forced out.

He can be tagged out while off a base.

And there are some less common ways. Baserunners must run within three feet of the basepaths unless he's avoiding interference with an opposing player who's fielding a ball. Otherwise, out! If he passes another runner or runs to a base already occupied . . . out! If a batted ball hits him (and the ball didn't pass by or "through" a fielder, and if it wasn't deflected off a fielder) . . . out! And if he (or a coach) interferes with a fielder making a play . . . out!

THE WORLD SERIES

Year	Winner	Loser
1903	Boston (A.L.) 5 wins	Pittsburgh (N.L.) 3 wins
1904	No Series	
1905	New York (N.L.) 4	Philadelphia (A.L.) 1
1906	Chicago (A.L.) 4	Chicago (N.L.) 2
1907	Chicago (N.L.) 4	Detroit (A.L.) 0; 1 tie
1908	Chicago (N.L.) 4	Detroit (A.L.) 1
1909	Pittsburgh (N.L.) 4	Detroit (A.L.) 3
1910	Philadelphia (A.L.) 4	Chicago (N.L.) 1
1911	Philadelphia (A.L.) 4	New York (N.L.) 2
1912	Boston (A.L.) 4	New York (N.L.) 3; 1 tie
1913	Philadelphia (A.L.) 4	New York (N.L.) 1
1914	Boston (N.L.) 4	Philadelphia (A.L.) 0
1915	Boston (A.L.) 4	Philadelphia (N.L.) 1
1916	Boston (A.L.) 4	Brooklyn (N.L.) 1
1917	Chicago (A.L.) 4	New York (N.L.) 2
1918	Boston (A.L.) 4	Chicago (N.L.) 2
1919	Cincinnati (N.L.) 5	Chicago (A.L.) 3
1920	Cleveland (A.L.) 5	Brooklyn (N.L.) 2
1921	New York (N.L.) 5	New York (A.L.) 3
1922	New York (N.L.) 4	New York (A.L.) 0; 1 tie
1923	New York (A.L.) 4	New York (N.L.) 2
1924	Washington (A.L.) 4	New York (N.L.) 3
1925	Pittsburgh (N.L.) 4	Washington (A.L.) 3
1926	St. Louis (N.L.) 4	New York (A.L.) 3
1927	New York (A.L.) 4	Pittsburgh (N.L.) 0
1928	New York (A.L.) 4	St. Louis (N.L.) 0
1929	Philadelphia (A.L.) 4	Chicago (N.L.) 1
1930	Philadelphia (A.L.) 4	St. Louis (N.L.) 2
1931	St. Louis (N.L.) 4	Philadelphia (A.L.) 3
1932	New York (A.L.) 4	Chicago (N.L.) 0
1933	New York (N.L.) 4	Washington (A.L.) 1
1934	St. Louis (N.L.) 4	Detroit (A.L.) 3
1935	Detroit (A.L.) 4	Chicago (N.L.) 2
1936	New York (A.L.) 4	New York (N.L.) 2
1937	New York (A.L.) 4	New York (N.L.) 1
1938	New York (A.L.) 4	Chicago (N.L.) 0
1939	New York (A.L.) 4	Cincinnati (N.L.) 0
1940	Cincinnati (N.L.) 4	Detroit (A.L.) 3
1941	New York (A.L.) 4	Brooklyn (N.L.) 1
1942	St. Louis (N.L.) 4	New York (A.L.) 1
1943	New York (A.L.) 4	St. Louis (N.L.) 1
1944	St. Louis (N.L.) 4	St. Louis (A.L.) 2

Year	Winner	Loser
1945	Detroit (A.L.) 4	Chicago (N.L.) 3
1946	St. Louis (N.L.) 4	Boston (A.L.) 3
1947	New York (A.L.) 4	Brooklyn (N.L.) 3
1948	Cleveland (A.L.) 4	Boston (N.L.) 2
1949	New York (A.L.) 4	Brooklyn (N.L.) 1
1950	New York (A.L.) 4	Philadelphia (N.L.) 0
1951	New York (A.L.) 4	New York (N.L.) 2
1952	New York (A.L.) 4	Brooklyn (N.L.) 3
1953	New York (A.L.) 4	Brooklyn (N.L.) 2
1954	New York (N.L.) 4	Cleveland (A.L.) 0
1955	Brooklyn (N.L.) 4	New York (A.L.) 3
1956	New York (A.L.) 4	Brooklyn (N.L.) 3
1957	Milwaukee (N.L.) 4	New York (A.L.) 3
1958	New York (A.L.) 4	Milwaukee (N.L.) 3
1959	Los Angeles (N.L.) 4	Chicago (A.L.) 2
1960	Pittsburgh (N.L.) 4	New York (A.L.) 3
1961	New York (A.L.) 4	Cincinnati (N.L.) 1
1962	New York (A.L.) 4	San Francisco (N.L.) 3
1963	Los Angeles (N.L.) 4	New York (A.L.) 0
1964	St. Louis (N.L.) 4	New York (A.L.) 3
1965	Los Angeles (N.L.) 4	Minnesota (A.L.) 3
1966	Baltimore (A.L.) 4	Los Angeles (N.L.) 0
1967	St. Louis (N.L.) 4	Boston (A.L.) 3
1968	Detroit (A.L.) 4	St. Louis (N.L.) 3
1969	New York (N.L.) 4	Baltimore (A.L.) 1
1970	Baltimore (A.L.) 4	Cincinnati (N.L.) 1
1971	Pittsburgh (N.L.) 4	Baltimore (A.L.) 3
1972	Oakland (A.L.) 4	Cincinnati (N.L.) 3
1973	Oakland (A.L.) 4	New York (N.L.) 3
1974	Oakland (A.L.) 4	Los Angeles (N.L.) 1
1975	Cincinnati (N.L.) 4	Boston (A.L.) 3
1976	Cincinnati (N.L.) 4	New York (A.L.) 0
1977	New York (A.L.) 4	Los Angeles (N.L.) 2
1978	New York (A.L.) 4	Los Angeles (N.L.) 2
1979	Pittsburgh (N.L.) 4	Baltimore (A.L.) 3
1980	Philadelphia (N.L.) 4	Kansas City (A.L.) 2
1981	Los Angeles (N.L.) 4	New York (A.L.) 2
1982	St. Louis (N.L.) 4	Milwaukee (A.L.) 3
1983	Baltimore (A.L.) 4	Philadelphia (N.L.) 1
1984	Detroit (A.L.) 4	San Diego (N.L.) 1
1985	Kansas City (A.L.) 4	St. Louis (N.L.) 3
1986	New York (N.L.) 4	Boston (A.L.) 3
1987	Minnesota (A.L.) 4	St. Louis (N.L.) 3

MEMBERS OF THE BASEBALL HALL OF FAME

(Listed by the year of their election)

1936
Ty Cobb
Walter Johnson
Christy Mathewson
Babe Ruth
Honus Wagner

1937
Napoleon Lajoie
Tris Speaker
Cy Young
Morgan Bulkeley
Ban Johnson
John McGraw
Connie Mack
George Wright

1938
Grover Cleveland
    Alexander
Alexander Cartwright
Henry Chadwick

1939
Eddie Collins
Lou Gehrig
Willie Keeler
George Sisler
Cap Anson
Charles Comiskey
Candy Cummings
Buck Ewing
Old Hoss Radbourne
Albert Spalding

1942
Rogers Hornsby

1944
Kenesaw Mountain
    Landis

1945
Roger Bresnahan
Dan Brouthers
Fred Clarke
Jimmy Collins
Ed Delahanty
Hugh Duffy
Hughie Jennings
King Kelly
Jim O'Rourke
Wilbert Robinson

1946
Jesse Burkett
Frank Chance
Jack Chesbro
Johnny Evers
Clark Griffith
Tommy McCarthy
Joe McGinnity
Eddie Plank
Joe Tinker
Rube Waddell
Ed Walsh

1947
Mickey Cochrane
Frankie Frisch
Lefty Grove
Carl Hubbell

1948
Herb Pennock
Pie Traynor

1949
Charlie Gehringer
Mordecai Brown
Kid Nichols

1951
Jimmie Foxx
Mel Ott

1952
Harry Heilmann
Paul Waner

1953
Dizzy Dean
Al Simmons
Edward Barrow
Chief Bender
Tom Connolly
Bill Klem
Bobby Wallace
Harry Wright

1954
Bill Dickey
Rabbit Maranville
Bill Terry

1955
Joe DiMaggio
Gabby Hartnett
Ted Lyons
Dazzy Vance
Home Run Baker
Ray Schalk

1956
Joe Cronin
Hank Greenberg

1957
Sam Crawford
Joe McCarthy

1959
Zach Wheat

1961
Max Carey
Billy Hamilton

1962
Bob Feller
Jackie Robinson
Bill McKechnie
Edd Roush

1963
John Clarkson
Elmer Flick
Sam Rice
Eppa Rixey

1964
Luke Appling
Red Faber
Burleigh Grimes
Miller Huggins
Tim Keefe
Heinie Manush
John Montgomery
   Ward

1965
Pud Galvin

1966
Ted Williams
Casey Stengel

1967
Red Ruffing
Branch Rickey
Lloyd Waner

1968
Joe Medwick
Kiki Cuyler
Goose Goslin

1969
Roy Campanella
Stan Musial
Stan Coveleski
Waite Hoyt

1970
Lou Boudreau
Earle Combs
Ford Frick
Jesse Haines

1971
Dave Bancroft
Jake Beckley
Chick Hafey
Harry Hooper
Joe Kelley
Rube Marquard
George Weiss
Satchel Paige

1972
Yogi Berra
Sandy Koufax
Early Wynn
Lefty Gomez
Will Harridge
Ross Youngs
Josh Gibson
Buck Leonard

1973
Roberto Clemente
Warren Spahn
Billy Evans
George Kelly
Mickey Welch
Monte Irvin

1974
Whitey Ford
Mickey Mantle
Jim Bottomley
Jocko Conlon
Sam Thompson
Cool Papa Bell

1975
Ralph Kiner
Earl Averill
Bucky Harris
Billy Herman
Judy Johnson

1976
Bob Lemon
Robin Roberts
Roger Connor
Cal Hubbard
Fred Lindstrom
Oscar Charleston

1977
Ernie Banks
Al Lopez
Joe Sewell
Amos Rusie
Martin Dihigo
Pop Lloyd

1978
Eddie Mathews
Addie Joss
Larry MacPhail

1979
Willie Mays
Warren Giles
Hack Wilson

1980
Al Kaline
Duke Snider
Chuck Klein
Tom Yawkey

1981
Bob Gibson
Rube Foster
Johnny Mize

1982
Hank Aaron
Frank Robinson
Happy Chandler
Travis Jackson

1983
Juan Marichal
Brooks Robinson
Walter Alston
George Kell

1984
Luis Aparicio
Don Drysdale
Harmon Killebrew
Rick Ferrell
Pee Wee Reese

1985
Hoyt Wilhelm
Lou Brock
Enos Slaughter
Arky Vaughn

1986
Willie McCovey
Bobby Doerr
Ernie Lombardi

1987
Catfish Hunter
Billy Williams
Ray Dandridge

1988
Willie Stargell

Recent Stars Soon to be Considered
Rod Carew
Tom Seaver
Jim Palmer
Johnny Bench
Carl Yastrzemski
Reggie Jackson
Pete Rose
Joe Morgan
Gaylord Perry
Phil Niekro
Steve Carlton
Don Sutton
Tony Perez
Nolan Ryan
Mike Schmidt

SINGLE-SEASON RECORDS

Batting and Baserunning (1900–1987)
Batting Average: .424, Rogers Hornsby, St. Louis (NL) 1924
Runs Scored: 177, Babe Ruth, New York (AL) 1921
Hits: 257, George Sisler, St. Louis (AL) 1920
Doubles: 67, Earl Webb, Boston (AL) 1931
Triples: 36, Owen Wilson, Pittsburgh (NL) 1912
Home Runs: 61, Roger Maris, New York (AL) 1961
Runs Batted In: 190, Hack Wilson, Chicago (NL) 1930
Stolen Bases: 130, Rickey Henderson, Oakland (AL) 1982

Pitching
Wins: 41, Jack Chesbro, New York (AL) 1904
Winning Percentage: .947, Elroy Face, Pittsburgh, (NL) 1959 (18–1 recor
Earned Run Average: 1.01, Dutch Leonard, Boston (AL) 1914
Games: 106, Mike Marshall, Los Angeles (NL) 1974
Strikeouts: 383, Nolan Ryan, California (AL) 1973
Shutouts: 16, Grover Alexander, Philadelphia (NL) 1916
Saves: 46, Dave Righetti, New York (AL) 1986

HOME RUN RECORDS

Most in a career: 755, Hank Aaron (1954–1976)

Most in a season: 61, Roger Maris (1961)

Most in a game: 4, Bobby Lowe (1984), Ed Delahanty (1896), Lou Gehrig (1932), Chuck Klein (1936), Pat Seery (1948), Gil Hodges (1950), Joe Adcock (1954), Rocky Colavito (1959), Willie Mays (1961), Mike Schmidt (1976), Bob Horner (1986)

Most by a pinch-hitter, career: 20, Cliff Johnson (1972–1984)

Most leading off a game, career: 35, Bobby Bonds (1968–1981)

Most by a rookie: 49, Mark McGwire (1987)

Most consecutive games hitting a homer: 8, Dale Long (1956), Don Mattingly (1987)

Most grand slam home runs, career: 23, Lou Gehrig (1923–1939)

Most grand slam home runs, season: 6, Don Mattingly (1987)

Most times leading the league in home runs: 12, Babe Ruth (1918–1921, 1923, 1924, 1926–1931)

Home run, 1st at-bat in major leagues: More than 50 different players.

Home run, 1st two at-bats in major leagues: Chuck Tanner (1955)

Home runs, one team, one game: 10, Toronto Blue Jays (1987)

Consecutive home runs, one inning, by a team: 4, Milwaukee Braves (1961), Cleveland Indians (1963), Minnesota Twins (1964)

Home runs, one team, one season: 240, New York Yankees (1961)

Home runs, two teammates, one season: 115, Roger Maris and Mickey Mantle, (1961)

Home runs, lifetime by a first baseman: 493, Lou Gehrig*

Home runs, lifetime by a second baseman: 266, Joe Morgan*

Home runs, lifetime by a third baseman: 491 Mike Schmidt*

Home runs, lifetime by a shortstop: 277, Ernie Banks*

Home runs, lifetime by an outfielder: 692, Babe Ruth*

Home runs, lifetime by a catcher: 327, Johnny Bench*

Home runs, lifetime by a pitcher: 36 Wes Ferrell*

*Total does not include home runs hit while playing other positions.

LIFETIME RECORDS (1900–1987)
Top Three

Games Played
Pete Rose (1963–1986) 3562
Carl Yastrzemski (1961–1983) 3308
Hank Aaron (1954–1976) 3298
Runs
Ty Cobb (1905–1928) 2245
Babe Ruth (1914–1935) 2174
Hank Aaron (1954–1976) 2174
Hits
Pete Rose (1963–1986) 4256
Ty Cobb (1905–1928) 4191
Hank Aaron (1954–1976) 3771
Doubles
Tris Speaker (1907–1928) 793
Pete Rose (1963–1986) 746
Stan Musial (1941–1963) 725
Triples
Sam Crawford (1900–1917) 304
Ty Cobb (1905–1928) 297
Honus Wagner (1900–1917) 231
Home Runs
Hank Aaron (1954–1976) 755
Babe Ruth (1914–1935) 714
Willie Mays (1951–1973) 660

Runs Batted In
Hank Aaron (1954–1976) 2297
Babe Ruth (1914–1935) 2211
Lou Gehrig (1923–1939) 1990
Stolen Bases
Lou Brock (1961–1979) 938
Ty Cobb (1905–1928) 892
Eddie Collins (1906–1930) 743
Walks
Babe Ruth (1914–1935) 2056
Ted Williams (1939–1960) 2019
Joe Morgan (1963–1984) 1865
Strikeouts
Reggie Jackson (1967–1987) 2597
Willie Stargell (1962–1982) 1936
Tony Perez (1964–1986) 1867
Total Bases
Hank Aaron (1954–1976) 6856
Stan Musial (1941–1963) 6134
Willie Mays (1951–1973) 6066
Batting Average
Ty Cobb (1905–1928) .367
Rogers Hornsby (1915–1937) .358
Joe Jackson (1908–1920) .356

LIFETIME RECORDS, PITCHING (1900–1987)
Top Three

Wins
Walter Johnson (1907–1927) 416
Christy Mathewson (1900–1916) 373
Grover Alexander (1911–1930) 373

Note: Cy Young is usually listed as the all-time win leader with 511, but he won only 246 games after 1900.

Games Pitched
Hoyt Wilhelm (1952–1972) 1070
Lindy McDaniel (1955–1975) 987
Rollie Fingers (1968–1985) 944

Complete Games
Walter Johnson (1907–1927) 531
Grover Alexander (1911–1930) 439
Christy Mathewson (1900–1916) 435
Innings Pitched
Walter Johnson (1907–1927) 5924
Gaylord Perry (1962–1983) 5351
Warren Spahn (1942–1965) 5244
Strikeouts
Nolan Ryan (1966–1987) 4547
Steve Carlton (1965–1987) 4131
Tom Seaver (1967–1986) 3640

Walks
Nolan Ryan (1966–1987) 2355
Early Wynn (1939–1963) 1775
Bob Feller (1936–1956) 1764
Shutouts
Walter Johnson (1907–1927) 110
Grover Alexander (1911–1930) 90
Christy Mathewson
  (1900–1916) 80

Saves
Rollie Fingers (1968–1985) 324
Goose Gossage (1972–1987) 289
Bruce Sutter (1976–1987) 286
Earned Run Average
Ed Walsh (1904–1917) 1.82
Addie Joss (1902–1910) 1.88
"Three Finger" Brown
  (1903–1916) 2.06

QUESTIONS AND ANSWERS

Why is the place where relief pitchers warm up called the bullpen?

In olden times, when many outfield walls were covered by advertising billboards (as they still are in the minor leagues), a chewing tobacco called Bull Durham was a common one. Many pitchers warmed up in front of the sign, and it came to be called a bullpen.

What is the difference between a full windup and a stretch?

With no one on base, pitchers deliver the ball from a full windup, bringing their arms over their head. With runners on base, they eliminate that step and work from a stretch position, hands at the belt. That prevents runners from getting an extra head start.

What happens when a batted ball bounces into the stands?

A fair ball into the stands on a bounce is called a ground-rule double. No runner can advance more than two bases.

What happens when a fan reaches over and touches the ball?
The umpire uses his judgment to decide how far the runners should advance.

Has any player ever had a mother who played professional baseball?
Believe it or not, yes! It wasn't the major leagues or the minor leagues, but it was the All-American Girls Professional Baseball League in the 1940s. Helen Callaghan was the player, and her son, Casey Candaele, broke in with the Montreal Expos in 1987.

What is the disabled list?
A player whose injury will sideline him for at least two weeks is put on the disabled list. He can be replaced by another player, often from the minor leagues, until he returns.

What are waivers?
This is a step teams take when they want to sell a player to another team. They "ask waivers" on a player and see if anyone else claims him. They can always withdraw the name, but waivers often lead to a player being released, particularly if no one claims him.

Why do managers have to wear uniforms?
No reason. It's just tradition. Connie Mack never wore one, nor did Brooklyn's Burt Shotten. But that was almost 40 years ago.

Which was the first team to put numbers on its uniforms?

The New York Yankees of 1929. The numbers were assigned to follow the usual batting order—#1 Earle Combs, #2 Mark Koenig, #3 Babe Ruth, #4 Lou Gehrig, etc.

Who has won the most MVP (Most Valuable Player) awards?

Seven players have won it three times: Jimmie Foxx, Joe DiMaggio, Mickey Mantle, Yogi Berra, Stan Musial, Roy Campanella, and Mike Schmidt.

Who has won both the Rookie of the Year Award and, later, the MVP Award?

Jackie Robinson, Frank Robinson, Rod Carew, Thurman Munson, Willie Mays, Don Newcombe, Orlando Cepeda, Willie McCovey, Pete Rose, Johnny Bench, and Fred Lynn. Lynn won them both in the same year (1975).

Who has won the most Cy Young awards as the league's best pitcher?

Steve Carlton won it four times.

Why is the ball so hard?

It's just the right size, weight, and shape for the field dimensions. It is designed so that it will go over the fence if hit just right, and stay in play if not. Like the distances between the bases, and from the pitcher to the catcher, it is one of the things about the game that is simply "just right."

Index

ABOUT THE AUTHOR

Marty Appel has been involved with baseball for more than 20 years—even longer if you count his days as a young fan collecting baseball cards. He has directed public relations for the New York Yankees and WPIX–TV, New York, where he now serves as Executive Producer of Yankee telecasts. He has also worked for former baseball commissioner Bowie Kuhn, both on his staff, and on his autobiography. Marty is the author and coauthor of many articles and books about baseball, including *Thurman Munson: An Autobiography* and *Tom Seaver's All-Time Baseball Greats.* He serves on the Advisory Committee to the annual Old-Timers' Baseball Classic and is a contributor to the *Encyclopedia Americana.* He lives in Larchmont, New York.